WEATHER

Grades 4-6

About This Book

This units focuses on temperature, wind, storms, air pressure, moisture and weather lore. Use the ideas and activities in this unit to supplement a theme on the weather in your classroom. 50 Activities.

Written by: Vi Clarke and Leona Melnyk
Illustrated by: S & S Learning Materials
Item #B1-60

Original Publication: 1991
Revision: 1999
©*1991 S & S Learning Materials*

Look For Other Science Units

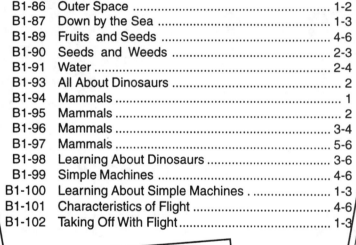

Published by:
S&S Learning Materials
15 Dairy Avenue
Napanee, Ontario
K7R 1M4

Distributed in U.S.A. by:
T4T Learning Materials
5 Columba Drive, Suite 175
Niagara Falls, New York
14385

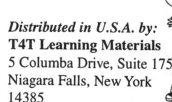

WEATHER

Table of Contents

Written by Vi Clarke and Leona Melnyk

ISBN 1-55035-222-9

WEATHER

Teacher Input Suggestions

1. Brainstorm for "weather" words. List the words on chart paper and/or a "cloud" shape. Words can pertain to forms of water (dew, rain, etc.), or wind (gale, breeze, etc.), or temperature. (balmy, chilly, etc.)

2. Clip the weather forecast from your daily newspaper for two or three weeks. Determine how often the forecasts are correct.

3. Make a scrapbook of newspaper stories about unusual weather or unusual effects of the weather.

4. Be a "cloud detective". Take photographs of different types of clouds. Make a picture chart of the different photographs. Try to determine the types of clouds. Label them.

5. If possible, plan a trip to a local weather station.

6. Invite a meteorologist to the classroom to demonstrate the use of various weather instruments.

7. Show filmstrips and or videos pertaining to the unit.

8. Have students interview people of different occupations to see how a weather forecast affects their jobs. Try to include a farmer, a fruit-grower, a manufacturer, a fisherman, a forester, and an aviator. Students will report on these interviews to the class and discuss the answers given. Perhaps the interviews could be taped.

9. Have a choral reading of weather poems e.g. "Weather" by Aileen Fisher, "Wind" by Aileen Fisher, "Without a Trumpet" by Vivian Gouled, "Understanding" by Myra Cohn Livingstone. Perhaps students could choose their favourite one to illustrate.

10. Students could make a collection of poems for each season. These could be put in booklet form.

WEATHER

11. Encourage reading with a book thermometer. Make a "thermometer" from bristol board with a red construction paper "bulb". To raise the "temperature" a student must read an entire book. This earns 3 cm of "mercury" on the thermometer. Put title, author, and name of the student who read it on each mercury segment. Set a class goal to reach the top by a certain date.

12. In a reading corner, make a rainbow shape from styrofoam and paint it using the colours of the spectrum. Colourful letters for the words "Reading Rainbow" could also be cut from styrofoam and mounted beside the rainbow shape.

13. Using weather balloon shapes, create a bulletin board display entitled "Float Away With a Good Book!" Write the title, the author, and the name of the student who read the book on the weather balloon basket.

Weather

List of Vocabulary

rotation, revolution, Celsius, Fahrenheit, solar, solar eclipse, sunscald, sunstone, sunfast, sunsnake, atmospheric, average, extreme, anemometer, chinook, haboob, willy-willy, sirocco, doldrums, monsoons, harmattan, foehn, eddies, Beaufort, acrostic, haiku, barometer, air pressure, tropical, polar, meteorologist, radiosonde, rain gauge, cirrus, cumulus, stratus, evaporation, condensation, precipitation, nephoscope, nimbus, cumulonimbus, spectrum, chlorofluorocarbons, methane, pollutants, ozone, environmental, occlusion, Coriolis force, horse latitudes, acid rain, sulfates, nitrates, hygrometer, wind vane, humidity

WEATHER

List of Resources

1. Branley, Franklyn M. **Flash, Crash, Rumble and Roll.** Ontario. Fitzhenry & Whiteside Ltd. © 1964

2. Dickinson, Terence. **Exploring the Sky by Day**. Ontario. Camden House © 1988

3. Dockery, Wallene T. **Weather or Not**. New York. Abingdon Press © 1976

4. Frodin, Dennis Brindell. **Disaster/Hurricanes**. Chicago. Children's Press © 1982

5. Frevert, Patricia Dendtler. **Why Does Weather Change?** Minnesota. Creative Education, Inc. © 1981

6. Hornstein, Reuben A. **The Forecast Your Own Weather Book**. Ontario. McClelland and Stewart Ltd. © 1980

7. Mitchell - Christie, Frank. **Practical Weather Forecasting**. New York. Barron's © 1978

8. Santrey Lawrence. **What makes the Wind?** New Jersey Troll Associates © 1982

9. Updegraff, Imelda and Robert. **Continents and Climates.** Minnesota. The Children's Book Company © 1981

10. Webster, Vera. **Weather Experiments**. Chicago. Children's Press © 1982

WEATHER

Name: _____

Record the number of each activity that you complete in the correct box.

Temperature	Wind	Air Pressure
Moisture	Storms	Weather Lore

"Snow-Foolin!"

_____ has completed

"sun"-sational work during our study of the weather!

Signed: _____

Date: _____

WEATHER

Temperature - Activity 1

The Earth's Tilt

Why are some parts of the earth heated much more than others? To understand this we have to consider how the earth moves. The earth rotates (turns) on its axis, an imaginary line that connects the North and South Poles, once every twenty-four hours. This spinning motion makes the sun appear to move from east to west and causes day and night on earth.

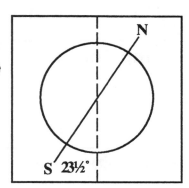

The sun is approximately 150 000 000 kilometres (93 000 000 miles) from earth. The earth revolves (goes around) the sun once every year. In 365 days the earth travels a distance of 958 million kilometres (595 million miles) around the sun. This path is called the earth's orbit. The tilt of the earth's axis and the earth's revolution around the sun cause the change in seasons. For half the year, the Northern Hemisphere is tilted toward the sun causing summer. For the other half of the year, the Northern Hemisphere is tilted away from the sun. That's when we have winter. The equator receives direct sunlight all year round.

A In order for you to further understand the earth's tilt in relation to the sun, fill two shoeboxes with soil and insert a thermometer to the same depth in each box. Take them outside in the sunlight. Let one box lie flat on the ground and prop the other box up so that its surface is facing the sun's rays more directly. Take four temperature readings every half hour and record your results on a chart like the example. Then write your conclusions below the chart.

WEATHER

Time	Temperature	
	Shoebox lying flat	**Shoebox propped up**

Conclusions:_____

_____

_____

B Using the information from the paragraphs copy and complete the following sentences.

1. The earth _____ or turns on its axis once every _____.

2. The earth's _____ around the sun once every _____ gives us our _____ - spring, summer, fall, and winter.

3. For part of the year, the _____ Hemisphere where we live, tilts away from the sun giving us _____.

4. The area of the earth known as the _____ receives very direct sunlight all year round.

5. The earth is about _____ km away from the sun.

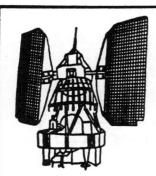 

WEATHER

Temperature - Activity 2

Some Like it Hot, Some Like it Cold

Did you know that the <u>highest</u> temperature ever recorded on earth was 58° C (136° F.) at Al Azizyah, Libya and that the <u>lowest</u> ever recorded was -88° C (-127° F) at Vostok in Antarctica? These are extremes. The average surface temperature on earth is 14° C (57° F).

In order to take temperatures, a <u>thermometer</u> is used to record temperature changes. Mercury is a metal that is used in this instrument. Metals expand when they are heated and contract when the temperature drops. The mercury is contained in a bulb at the end of a long narrow glass tube. When the temperature rises, the mercury expands in the bulb and is pushed up the tube. A scale is marked on the thermometer showing the degrees of temperature rise. The two most common temperature scales used on thermometers are Celsius and Fahrenheit. At very low temperatures alcohol, not mercury, is used because it has a lower freezing point.

Do a little research and find out the following temperatures. Using a red pencil, shade in the temperatures on the thermometers.

1. the freezing point of water
2. the boiling point of water
3. a comfortable indoor temperature
4. the temperature outside on a warm sunny day
5. today's temperature

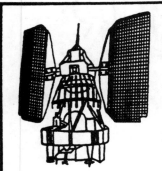

WEATHER

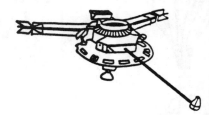

| 1 | 2 | 3 | 4 | 5 |

212 — 100 212 — 100 212 — 100 212 — 100 212 — 100
— 90   — 90   — 90   — 90   — 90
— 80   — 80   — 80   — 80   — 80
— 70   — 70   — 70   — 70   — 70
— 60   — 60   — 60   — 60   — 60
— 50   — 50   — 50   — 50   — 50
— 40   — 40   — 40   — 40   — 40
— 30   — 30   — 30   — 30   — 30
— 20   — 20   — 20   — 20   — 20
— 10   — 10   — 10   — 10   — 10
32 — 0   32 — 0   32 — 0   32 — 0   32 — 0
— -10   — -10   — -10   — -10   — -10
— -20   — -20   — -20   — -20   — -20

Answer these questions:

1. Why is water not a useful liquid for thermometers?

_____

_____

2. Would you use alcohol or mercury in a thermometer if you wanted to measure temperatures at the North Pole?_____

   Tell why._____

WEATHER

Temperature - Activity 3

Environmental Issues

Over the past while there has been an enormous amount of talk with relation to our environment and, more specifically, "The Greenhouse Effect". You may be somewhat puzzled as to what this "Greenhouse Effect" actually is. To increase your awareness and knowledge read the information that follows.

As heat from the sun enters our atmosphere a certain percentage is reflected back into space mostly by the clouds. But close to 50% of the sunlight reaches the earth's surface to heat the land and waters. Heat then comes from the land and waters to warm the atmosphere. The atmosphere absorbs the heat and it is prevented from passing back into space because of the buildup of carbon dioxide and other gases such as chlorofluorocarbons (CFC's) and methane. These gases act like the glass in a greenhouse. A greenhouse is a building made basically from glass where plants can be grown all year round because the greenhouse allows the sunlight in but prevents the heat from escaping. Likewise, the sun's heat in our atmosphere is trapped by gases.

The carbon dioxide and other gases are the direct result of human activities. Exhaust from cars and other modes of transportation, smog pouring from the smokestacks of factories, the gases released from residential and commercial heating - all contribute to this deplorable problem. The excessive chopping of trees also aggravates the issue because trees absorb a lot of carbon dioxide.

Scientists warn us about this global warming, as it's referred to. Our planet is gradually "heating" up. If it continues it can eventually lead to widespread drought and the melting of the polar ice cap could cause coastal flooding. Generally speaking most authorities believe that it is essential that we all work together to rectify this problem. Governments are approaching

WEATHER

Manufacturers and Industries to encourage the reduction of pollutants released into the atmosphere.

The CFC's are also being blamed for the deterioration of the ozone layer. The ozone layer is a layer of gas called "ozone" that protects the Earth from nearly 90% of the sun's ultraviolet rays. In the late 1970's some scientists found a hole in the ozone layer over the Antarctica region. Since then, the problem has gotten progressively worse. Exposure to an overabundance of ultraviolet rays can lead to all kinds of problems - from severe sunburn to skin cancer. In 1987 a treaty was signed by forty countries to take action against CFC's. One common source of CFC's is the use of aerosol spray cans.

A We all have a responsibility to clean up our environment. In the garbage cans below write six ways you can help with these environmental issues.

B On a T-shirt shape create an illustration and slogan which will encourage people to become more conscious of environmental issues. (i.e. banning aerosol cans, plastics, recycling, the greenhouse effect, the ozone crisis, etc.) "Whether" we save our planet or not is up to us.

TREES

ARE A

GROWING

CONCERN

PLANT ONE TODAY!

WEATHER

Temperature - Activity 4

Temperatures Rising

Is your temperature rising because it has rained for 14 days straight and you're angry and fed up?

Is the recorded outside temperature rising so high that you're having difficulty cooling off?

If you live in a climate where temperatures are bitter cold in winter, you can understand why people wait in anticipation for the first sign of warm weather. In such climates, the weather is often a daily topic of conversation. But what would it be like to live in a hot, sultry <u>desert</u>, or in the <u>jungles of Africa</u>, or perhaps far north in the <u>Arctic regions</u>? The temperature affects our moods, our choice of clothing, our jobs and our overall lifestyle.

Pretend you were sent to one of the three regions underlined above. Explain how your life would change. What would be your biggest adjustment? What would be the advantages of living there? What would be the disadvantages? Would you choose to stay there permanently or would you try to return to your former home? Tell the story of your adventure.

Accompany your story with three pictures of yourself in your new environment. Use the picture frames provided to do your illustrations. Write a few lines about each picture.

1.

_____

_____

_____

_____

_____

_____

WEATHER

2.

_____

_____

_____

_____

_____

_____

3.

_____

_____

_____

_____

_____

_____

WEATHER

Temperature - Activity 5

Solar Power

The word <u>solar</u> means pertaining to the sun.

<u>Solar energy</u> is energy given off by the sun.

<u>Solar eclipses</u> occur when the moon's shadow sweeps across the face of the earth. A total eclipse occurs if the moon completely blots out the sun. A partial eclipse occurs if the moon covers only part of the sun.

The <u>solar system</u> consists of the sun and the heavenly bodies whose motions are directly or indirectly determined by the sun.

Listed below are several "sun" words. Have some "fun" shine as you try to match the words in **Column A** with their meanings in **Column B**.

<u>Column A</u>

1. sunspot
2. sunwise
3. sunstone
4. sundog
5. sundial
6. sunshade
7. sunroof
8. sunscald
9. sunsnake
10. sunfast

<u>Column B</u>

___ a protection from the sun

___ an injury of woody plants caused by the sun

___ a small rainbow

___ resistant to fading by the sun

___ a dark patch observed on the sun's surface

___ from left to right

___ a type of time-telling device

___ an automobile roof having a panel that opens

___ a variety of quartz

___ an ornament found in Northern European art, shaped like an S, with a small circle in the centre.

Find two more "sun"-sational words of your own. Write their meanings.

_____   _____

WEATHER

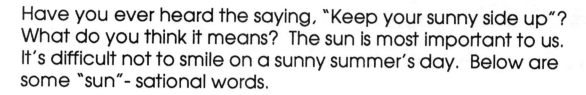

Just "Sun" - sational

Have you ever heard the saying, "Keep your sunny side up"?
What do you think it means? The sun is most important to us.
It's difficult not to smile on a sunny summer's day. Below are
some "sun"- sational words.

A First put the list in alphabetical order.

sunbonnet   _____

sunny   _____

sunset   _____

sunbeam   _____

Sunday   _____

sunshine   _____

sunflower   _____

sunrise   _____

sunburn   _____

B Now use some of these words to create two of your own
"sun" - sational poems. On scrap paper write a limerick
and a cinquain. Select your favourite poem and write it
on the sun shape provided. (see examples)

Limericks

A limerick is an amusing poem consisting of five lines. The first,
second and fifth lines rhyme with each other, the third and
fourth lines rhyme.

For example: **Once on a sunny Autumn day,
A farmer decided to harvest the hay,
All seemed to go well
Til! the farmer suddenly fell,
Now he's in a cast until May.**

WEATHER

Cinquains

A Cinquain is a poem with five lines. This pattern is followed when writing a cinquain.

Line 1 - one word to name your topic
Line 2 - two words describing your topic
Line 3 - three action words
Line 4 - a four word phrase
Line 5 - states another word for the title

For example:

Sun
Hot, Bright
Blazes, Beams, Burns
Reminds me of summer
Fireball

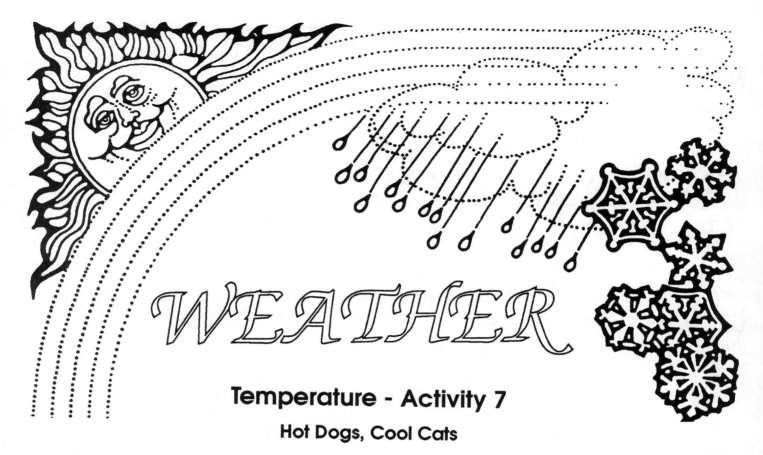

Temperature - Activity 7

Hot Dogs, Cool Cats

Summertime can be great fun for your pet. You are on vacation from school and have a lot of time to devote to your cat or dog. It is important, however, to beware of hot weather hazards. These range from pesky fleas to deadly heatstroke.

Write a list of do's and don'ts for your friends so they will be aware of things to do in order to help their feline or canine stay healthy in warm weather. Try to make a list of 8 tips.

e.g.

Do not leave your pet alone in the car.

WEATHER

Temperature - Activity 8

Mapping the Weather

According to <u>The Kids World Almanac</u> (1985 edition) some world weather extremes are charted below.

A Read the chart carefully. Then using an atlas locate each place mentioned and label it on the map provided.

Extreme	Place	Factual Information
sunniest	Sahara Desert	sunshine 97% of the time
coldest	Plateau Station, Antarctica	average yearly temperature -70°F (-21°C)
coldest inhabited spot	Oymyakon, Siberia	-97°F (-36°C) in 1964
rainiest	Mt. Waialeale, Hawaii	annual average rainfall 460 in. (924 cm)
driest	Atacoma Desert, Chile	less than 1.5 in. (3.3cm) of rain in one year
windiest	Mt. Washington, New Hampshire, U.S.A.	1934 - a world record wind of 231 mph (370 kph)
coldest recorded temperature	Vostok, Antarctica	-127°F (-88°C) on Aug. 24, 1960
hottest recorded temperature	Al Azizyah, Libya	136°F (58°C) on Sept. 13 1922
greatest 1 day rainfall	Cilaos, La Reunion Indian Ocean	72.62 in. (159.76 cm) on March 15-16, 1952
longest hot spell	Marble Bar, Australia	162 consecutive days of 100°F (38°C)

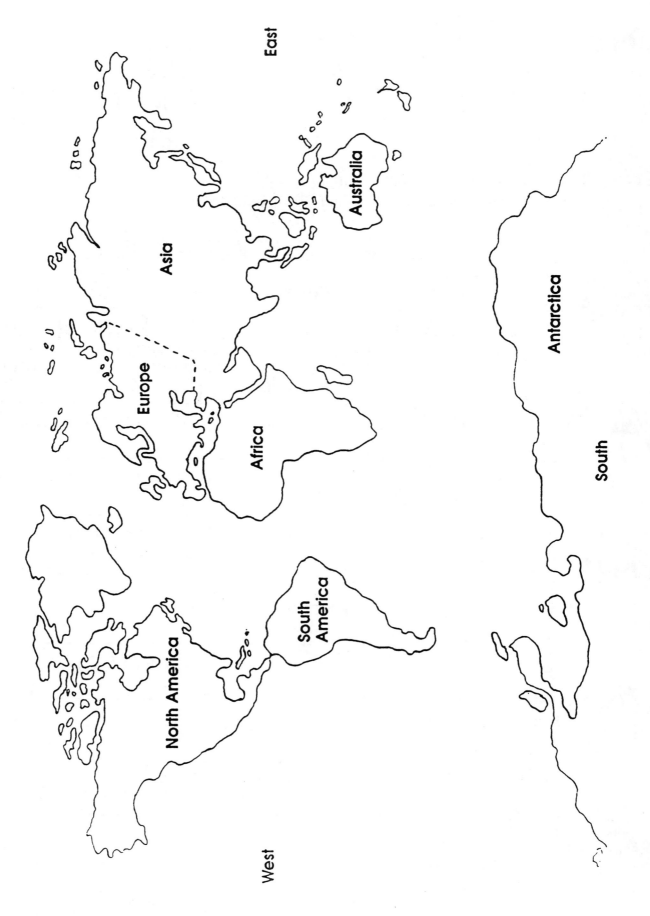

North

East

Asia

Australia

Europe

Africa

Antarctica

South

North America

South America

West

WEATHER

B The magic genie that lives inside this urn has given you the chance to take a trip to any three of the places that you located on the map. Which places would you choose? Why? Tell the story of your journey on the lines provided.

Dry?   Rainy?   Hot?   Cold?   Windy?

_____
_____
_____
_____
_____
_____
_____
_____
_____
_____
_____
_____
_____

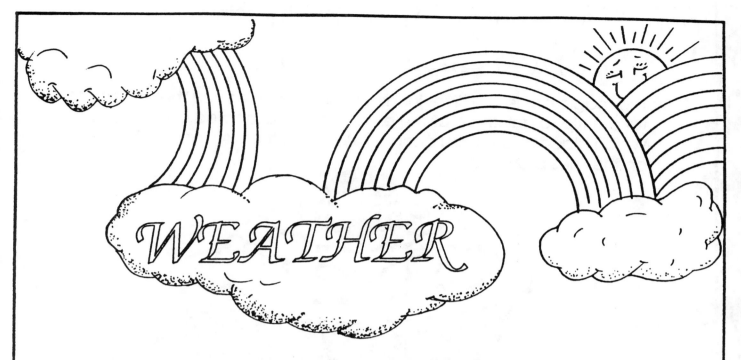

Temperature - Activity 9

Weather Watch

Some days are hot and sultry, while others are windy, cold or sometimes rainy or snowy. Using the calendar provided, record the temperature each day at the same time for one month. Be sure to place your thermometer in the shade so that you measure air temperature and not the effects of the sun's heat. Number the days of the month in the right hand corner of the calendar. In the left triangle record the temperature and in the centre draw a weather symbol for each day. For example:

SUNNY   **CLOUDY**   **SNOWY**   **RAINY and CLOUDY**

At the end of the month do the following:

    (a) find the <u>average</u> temperature for that month

    (b) give the fraction that would represent:

              (1) the number of sunny days _____
              (2) the number of cloudy days (no rain) _____
              (3) the number of snowy days _____
              (4) the number of rainy and cloudy days _____

Sun.	Mon.	Tues.	Wed.	Thurs.	Fri.	Sat.

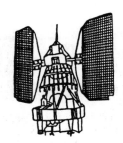
WEATHER

Temperature - Activity 10

Reading a Weather Map

A Below you will find symbols which are frequently and commonly used on weather maps. Do some research and see if you can match the symbol with its appropriate interpretation. The first one is done for you.

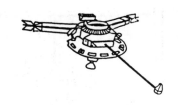

steady, heavy rain	light snow shower	lightning	mist
	H	L	

Answers to choose from: quasi-stationary front, centre of high pressure, continuous precipitation, occlusion, cold front, centre of low pressure, warm front, light thunderstorm with rain, fog, intermittent light drizzle, steady light snow, mist, lightning, light snow shower, intermittent moderate snow, intermittent light rain, steady heavy rain, steady light drizzle, heavy thunderstorm, light rain shower.

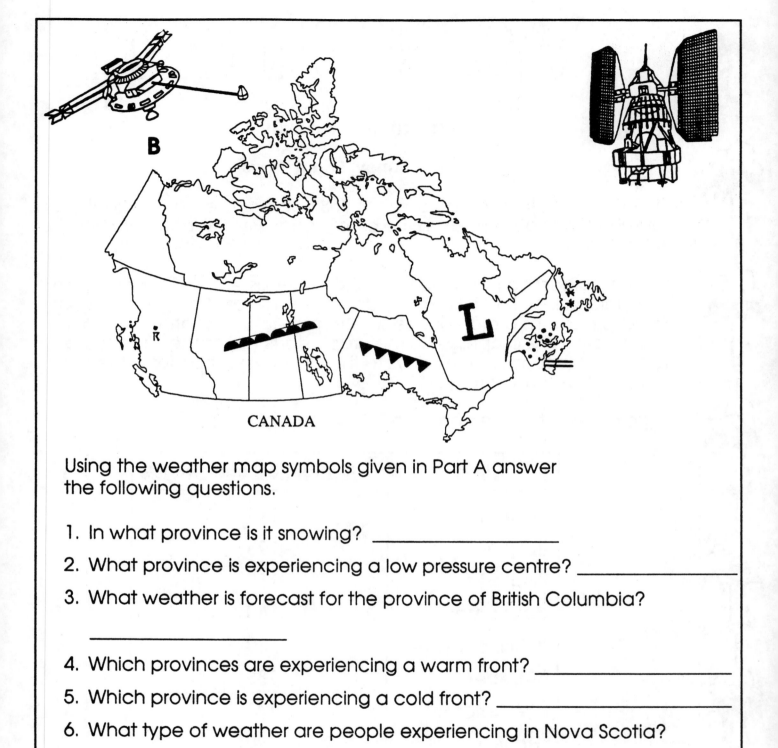

B

CANADA

Using the weather map symbols given in Part A answer the following questions.

1. In what province is it snowing? _____

2. What province is experiencing a low pressure centre? _____

3. What weather is forecast for the province of British Columbia?

   _____

4. Which provinces are experiencing a warm front? _____

5. Which province is experiencing a cold front? _____

6. What type of weather are people experiencing in Nova Scotia?

   _____

7. Which two provinces are having steady heavy rain?

   _____

WEATHER

Temperature - Activity 11

Sunny, Sunny, Sunny Days

St. Petersburg, Florida can boast of 768 consecutive days of continuous sunshine. The South Pole, on the other hand, went without sunshine for 182 days!

We in Canada do not have these extremes. Listed below are certain Canadian cities and how many days the sun was shining in one year. Because graphs are a concise way to present information, let's put this data on the graph. Fill in the graph starting with the city having the least number of sunny days to the city having the most. The first one has been done for you.

Then answer the questions that follow the graph.

<u>Cities</u>	<u>Number of Sunny Days</u>
St. John's	110
Regina	195
Victoria	165
Edmonton	180
Charlottetown	130
Quebec	185
Fredericton	145
Halifax	120
Winnipeg	200
Ottawa	190

WEATHER

Sunny Days in One Year in Canadian Cities

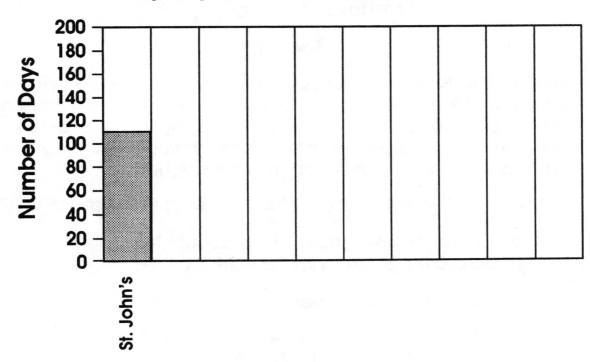

Number of Days

200
180
160
140
120
100
80
60
40
20
0

St. John's

Cities

Questions to answer:

1. Which city had the greatest number of sunny days? _____

2. Which city had the least number of sunny days? _____

3. Give the number of days that were <u>not</u> sunny out of 365 days that year for the following cities:

       (a) Winnipeg   _____ days
       (b) Quebec   _____ days
       (c) Fredericton   _____ days
       (d) Halifax   _____ days
       (e) Charlottetown _____ days

WEATHER

Temperature - Activity 12

Far Out!

Would it be hot enough for you in Midale Saskatchewan where the temperature reached 45°C on July 5, 1937? Or perhaps you would prefer to be cool. It was -63°C (-81°F) at Snag in the Yukon on February 3, 1947. These extreme temperatures on Earth are mild compared to temperatures on the other planets.

If you like the heat, try living on Venus - Venus sizzles at 455°C (850°F)!

Looking for somewhere cooler? How about Mars where the temperature can be as low as -124°C (-191°F)?

The weather on planets depends on three things:

1. the distance from the sun
2. the atmosphere
3. the rotation of the planet

Because of its atmospheric conditions, rotation, and distance from the sun, Earth's weather is out of this world!

A Listed below are the planets in order from the shortest to the greatest distance from the sun. Do some research and record the temperatures for each planet.

Mercury _____   Saturn _____

Venus _____   Uranus _____

Earth _____   Neptune _____

Mars _____   Pluto _____

Jupiter _____

B Draw a scene depicting vegetation or perhaps life (human or otherwise) that would exist on one of the planets other than Earth. Make your drawing far out!

WEATHER

Temperature - Activity 13

How To Make a Thermometer

A thermometer is a specific instrument used to measure how hot or cold something is. We can measure the air on a hot summer's day; we can measure body temperature or even the water temperature of a swimming pool. Thermometers are used in numerous ways.

To make your very own thermometer, first assemble the materials listed below. (Perhaps this will be a teacher directed demonstration lesson.)

Materials needed:

1. a narrow necked bottle (a small soda bottle works well)

2. a straw

3. some clay

4. food colouring

5. a hot plate

6. water

7. a pot

8. ice cubes

9. an oven mitt

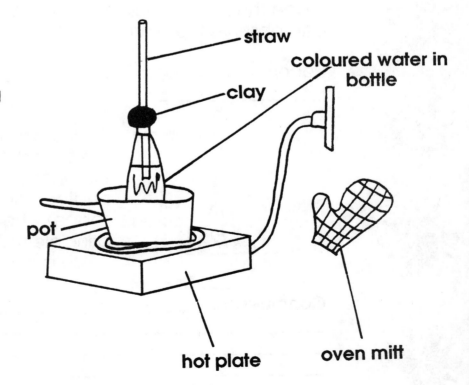

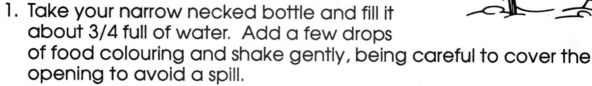

WEATHER

Procedure:

1. Take your narrow necked bottle and fill it about 3/4 full of water. Add a few drops of food colouring and shake gently, being careful to cover the opening to avoid a spill.

2. Place a straw in the bottle submerging one end in the coloured water. Use clay to hold the straw in place. It is <u>essential</u> that there is an <u>airtight seal</u> between the <u>straw</u> and the <u>bottle</u> so be sure to mold the clay carefully. **PRESS FIRMLY**.

3. Now put your bottle in a pot of water and place it on a hot plate. Heat the water in the pot to the boiling point.

   Record what happens now. _____
   _____

4. Next remove the bottle from the pot. Use an oven mitt so you don't burn yourself. Allow the bottle to cool somewhat. Now place the bottle back in the pot. Surround it with ice cubes and observe the results.

   Record what happens now. _____

straw

ice cubes

pot

As you already know, thermometers are based on the principle that matter expands (takes up more space) when heated and contracts (takes up less space) when cooled. Recalling this principle write your conclusions to these activities.

Conclusions:_____
_____
_____
_____

WEATHER

Wind - Activity 1

Wind Belts

Air is constantly on the move. Warm air rises and cold air moves down. This movement of air from a high pressure area to a low pressure area causes the WIND to blow. The greater the difference in pressure between the two areas, the fiercer the wind will be.

The sun plays a very vital role in these movements. The sun heats the earth unevenly. For example, the equator is always very hot because the sun's rays shine directly down at it. However, the sun's rays hit the remainder of the earth at varying degrees or angles. Because the earth rotates from west to east, winds blowing toward the equator have a tendency to curve toward the east. This is known as Coriolis force. Due to this force, the general circulation of the atmosphere is made up of winds that go around the earth in wind bands called wind belts. There are six of these wind belts.

A Using an encyclopedia or other appropriate reference materials, find out the names of the six belts and label the globe shape provided. Then read the statements in Part B and from your research see if you can fill in the blanks with the correct responses.

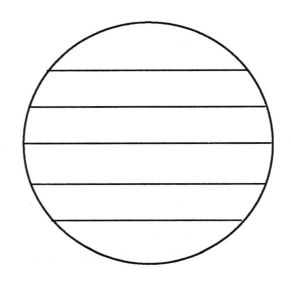

Wind Belts

WEATHER

B <u>Fill in the blanks:</u>

1. The westerlies are just another name for the _____
   _____

2. The _____ _____ were so named
   because of the early sailors who depended on these winds
   to do their business.

3. The region around the equator is sometimes referred to as the
   _____ because there are no winds.

4. Horse latitudes are_____
   _____

5. You live in the _____ or _____
   belt.

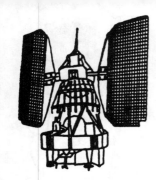

WEATHER

Wind - Activity 2

Blowing in the Wind

Wind is the movement of air over the earth's surface. Wind can blow slowly and gently or it may blow so hard and fast that it smashes buildings and pushes over large trees. Wind is a part of weather.

Local winds arise only in specific areas on the earth. For instance, chinooks are warm winds that blow down the side of a mountain. In Alberta, Canada, a chinook can raise the temperature by 20°C (36°F) in just a few minutes. In Southern California in the United States, there is a hot dry wind called the witch's wind, or Santa Ana, which can keep brush fires burning for days. In the Sudan, there is a strong wind called the haboob which whips up sandstorms. In Australia there is a hurricane called the willy-willy.

In the kite shapes which follow are names of more local winds as well as other words related to the wind. Using a dictionary or reference book write the meaning of each word.

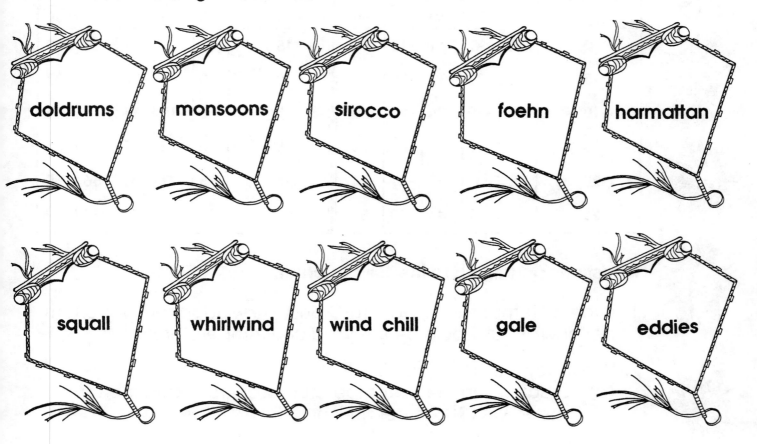

doldrums

monsoons

sirocco

foehn

harmattan

squall

whirlwind

wind chill

gale

eddies

Wind - Activity 3

The Big Chill

Very often on a cold, blustery winter's day, we hear the weather forecaster make mention of the wind chill factor. What does it mean? What actually happens is that the air temperature and the wind combine to make the air feel colder than the actual temperature reading. As an example, if the outside temperature was -10°C (14°F) and the wind speed was 20 kmh (12 mph) the wind chill would make it feel like the temperature was -19°C (-1°F)

You have been given 2 wind chill charts; one in Celsius; the other in Fahrenheit. Using the one best suited to your needs, answer the appropriate questions that follow the charts.

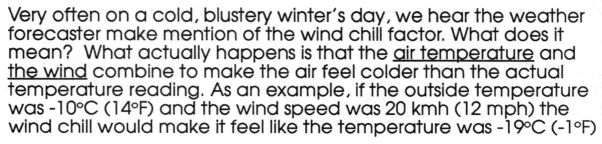

Wind Chill Temperatures (°C)						Wind Chill Temperature (°F)					
Air temperature (°C)	Wind Speed in km per hour					Air temperature (°F)	Wind Speed in miles per hour				
	10	20	30	40	50		0	10	20	30	40
0	-2	-7	-11	-13	-15	15	15	-3	-17	-25	-29
-5	-7	-13	-17	-20	-22	10	10	-9	-24	-33	-37
-10	-12	-19	-24	-27	-29	5	5	-15	-31	-41	-45
-15	-17	-25	-31	-34	-36	0	0	-22	-39	-49	-53
-20	-22	-31	-37	-41	-44	-5	-5	-27	-46	-56	-60
-25	-27	-37	-44	-48	-51	-10	-10	-34	-53	-64	-69

Questions pertaining to the Celsius chart:

1. If the air temperature was -10°C and the wind speed was 30 km per hour, what would be the wind chill temperature?

2. What day would be colder
   (a) a day when the air temperature was -15°C and the wind speed was 10 km per hour or

© 1991 S&S Learning Materials Limited

34

WEATHER

(b) a day when the air temperature was -5°C and the wind speed was 50 km per hour?

3. If the wind chill temperature was -41°C what would the air temperature and the wind speed be?

4. Studying the chart carefully tell what the air temperature and wind speed would be on

    (a) the coldest possible day
    (b) the warmest possible day.

5. Fill in the wind chill temperatures for the following readings:

Air Temperature	Wind Speed	Wind Chill Temperature
-10°C	30 km/h	_____
-25°C	20 km/h	_____
-15°C	10 km/h	_____
0°C	50 km/h	_____
-20°C	40 km/h	_____

Questions pertaining to the Fahrenheit chart:

1. If the air temperature was 10°F and the wind speed was 30 mph, what would be the wind chill temperature?

2. What day would be colder:
    (a) a day when the air temperature was 15°F and the wind speed was 40 mph **or**
    (b) a day when the air temperature was -10°F and the wind speed was 20 mph?

3. If the wind chill temperature was -46°F, what would the air temperature and the wind speed be?

WEATHER

4. Studying the chart carefully tell what the air temperature and wind speed would be on
   (a) the coldest possible day
   (b) the warmest possible day.

5. Fill in the wind chill temperature for the following readings:

Air temperature	Wind Speed	Wind Chill Temperature
5°F	20 mph	_____
-5°F	10 mph	_____
10°F	30 mph	_____
15°F	40 mph	_____
0°F	30 mph	_____

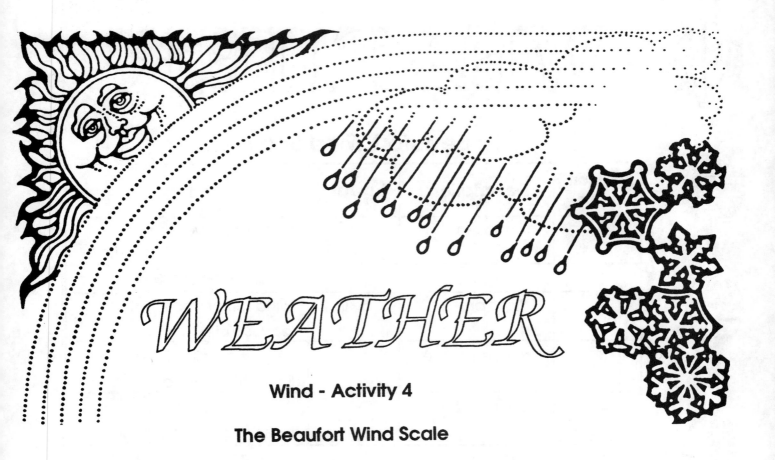

Wind - Activity 4

The Beaufort Wind Scale

In 1805 an Englishman named Sir Francis Beaufort devised the Beaufort wind scale. The scale is a series of numbers ranging from 0 to 17 that are used to indicate wind speeds. Wind speed is a feature of wind that is used in forecasting weather. In most countries, including Canada, wind speeds are measured in kilometres per hour while in the United States they are stated in miles per hour.

Look at the Beaufort wind scale to see the effect the winds have on land. Then do this activity:

Divide a piece of paper 21 cm x 28 cm (8 1/2" x 11") into four equal parts. Illustrate four of the winds from Beaufort's scale showing their effect on land. Be creative. Tell what number or write a description for those you illustrate.

Have fun. It can be a breeze!

WEATHER

Beaufort Wind Scale

Beaufort Number	Description	km/h	Effect on land
0	calm	less than 1	Smoke rises vertically
1	light air	1- 5	Smoke drifts with air
2	light breeze	6 - 11	Wind felt on face; leaves rustle
3	gentle breeze	12 - 19	Leaves, small twigs move; light flags extend.
4	moderate breeze	20 - 28	Small branches sway; dust, loose paper blow about
5	fresh breeze	29 - 38	Small trees sway; waves break on inland waters
6	strong breeze	39 - 49	Large branches sway; difficult to use umbrellas
7	moderate gale	50 - 61	Whole trees sway; difficult to walk against wind
8	fresh gale	62 - 74	Twigs broken off trees; very difficult walking against wind
9	strong gale	75 - 88	Slight damage to buildings; shingles may blow off roof
10	whole gale	89 - 102	Trees uprooted; considerable damage to buildings
11	storm	103 - 117	Widespread damage
12 - 17	hurricane	more than 117	Violent destruction

WEATHER

Wind - Activity 5

It's a Breeze

When the air around us alters from cold to hot and vice versa the air moves and this movement is called the wind. Winds affect our weather a great deal. If you watch a flag blowing in the breeze you can judge from which direction the wind is blowing. North winds are cold while south winds usually mean warm weather. East winds often mean a cloudy day is in store. West winds are usually warm and we can be somewhat certain of blue skies. The flags that follow are all blowing toward the west.

Carefully read the facts in each flag. Then tell whether the facts are True or False. Be sure to do a good job. With a little research, it'll be a breeze! (NOTE: If the answers are false, write the truth on lined paper.)

What city is known as the windy city?
Answer: Chicago

1. Wind is caused by the uneven heating of the air around the earth by energy from the sun. ( )

2. Local winds occur only in one place. ( )

3. Trade winds blow straight towards the equator. ( )

4. Wind speed is measured by an instrument called an anemometer. ( )

5. Wind direction is measured by an instrument called a weather guard. ( )

6. The Beaufort wind scale is a series of numbers that are used to indicate the various wind speeds. ( )

7. A warm, dry local wind that blows down the side of a mountain is called a chinook. ( )

8. In Europe a chinook is better known as a foehn. ( )

9. Helium-filled balloons are never used to measure winds. ( )

WEATHER

Wind - Activity 6

High Flying Poems

An <u>acrostic</u> is a poem or series of lines in which the first letters of each line form the name of something.

For example:

W - ind is air
I - n motion
N - orth, south, east, and west are the
D - irections from which the wind blows.

A **haiku** is a Japanese poem consisting of 3 lines with a total of 17 syllables.

Line 1 - 5 syllables
Line 2 - 7 syllables
Line 3 - 5 syllables

This type of poem is usually written about things in nature.
For example:

The wind blows calmly
Across the gentle water
On a clear morning.

Write a poem about wind following one of the above patterns. When it has been edited, write the final "draft" on a kite shape. Perhaps your poem can be displayed on a bulletin board under the heading "High Flying Poems."

Wind - Activity 7

A Chill Down My Spine

I wasn't usually afraid of the weather. Tonight, however, as I lay in bed I heard the window rattling madly in the wind. Outside my window I could see the trees swaying in the frenzied lashing of the wind. Behind the trees clouds scudded frantically across the blackened night sky. Every so often the moon ripped through them, creating eerie shadows. The house shook. Wind blew in the crevices around the window frame. I could hear the wind howling in the chimney. "I'm not afraid. I'm not afraid," I told myself. Suddenly I heard a crash!

What was it?

Who caused it?

Were you alone in the house?

Did the storm have an effect on the power? on the telephone?

Use your imagination and write a creative ending for this story beginning.

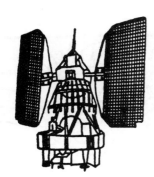
WEATHER

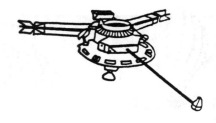

Wind- Activity 8

Measuring Wind Direction

As you know wind is the result of air in motion. Air is always moving from high pressure areas to low pressure areas. The strength of the wind is directly related to the differences in these pressures. Because temperature is what causes these changing air pressures, the sun is the main cause of the wind. Weather changes occur depending on the direction of the wind. A west wind comes from the west; an east wind comes from the east and so on.

Meteorologists use an instrument called a wind vane to measure wind direction. To make your very own wind vane follow the directions given.

Materials needed: a straw, a pencil, cardboard, stick pin, construction paper or ticket board

Method:

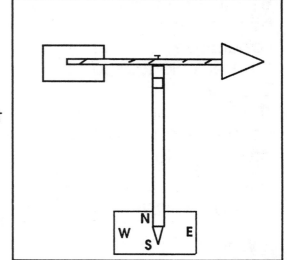

1. From cardboard or corrugated paper, cut a square 8 cm on each side to form a base. Mark the base -

	N	
W		E
	S	

2. Stick the sharpened end of the pencil into the center of the base.

3. Next, put a stick pin through the straw about 7 cm from 1 end. The straw should extend farther from the pivot at one end to allow the wind force to have its greatest effect.

4. Then continue to push the stick pin into the eraser of the pencil.

5. Tape an arrow made from construction paper or ticket board to the short end of the straw and a tail to the other end. (see diagram)

6. Put the wind vane in an open area and watch the straw rotate around the pin. In which direction is the wind blowing?

WEATHER

Wind - Activity 9

Measuring Wind Speed

The Beaufort wind scale is one way to estimate the speed of the wind by observing the wind's effect on smoke, leaves, branches of trees, flags flying, etc. A more reliable method is to use an anemometer, an instrument for measuring wind speed. Below is one method for constructing this weather instrument.

Materials needed:

1 empty thread spool
1 10 cm (4 inch) nail to fit inside the spool
4 styrofoam cups (Leave 3 white. <u>Paint</u> 1 the colour of your choice.)
4 .5 cm (1/4 inch) dowels (round sticks) 30 cm (12 in.) long
1-2 m (6 feet) long piece of wood on which to mount
  your anemometer

Activity:

1. Ask an adult to drill 4 .5 cm (1/4 in.) holes about half way up the spool, one on each side.

2. Put glue on the end of the 4 dowels and push them into the 4 holes of the spool.

3. Push the other end of the 4 dowels into the 4 styrofoam cups about 4 cm (1 1/2 in.) from the top. Push them through the outside of the cups about .5 cm (1/4 inch). The mouth of the cups should all point in the same direction. Put glue around the dowels where they meet the cups.

4. Using the nail, loosely fasten the spool to the piece of wood.

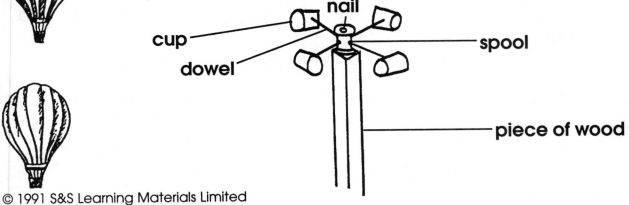

WEATHER

Your anemometer should now help you determine how fast the wind is blowing. Count the number of complete turns the painted cup makes in 30 seconds. Divide that number by 3 to give you the speed of wind in kilometres per hour. (Divide by 5 for the speed in miles per hour.)

How does the wind measure up in your neighbourhood today?

Is it calm or does it have the force of a hurricane?

Try your weather instrument and find out.

WEATHER

Air Pressure - Activity 1

Air Exerts Pressure

<u>Important</u>: Because the use of heat is involved, it is strongly suggested that the following two activities be carried out under teacher supervision or that they be done as a teacher demonstration lesson.

<u>Activities</u>

Have you ever felt your ears "pop" as you travelled in a car from a low elevation to a high elevation? This "popping" is caused by a change of air pressure against your body. Air pressure decreases with elevation.

The following two activities can be used to demonstrate the existence of air pressure. After completing the activities, answer the questions.

<u>Activity 1</u> - The Amazing Metal Can

<u>Materials needed</u>:

   1   empty metal can with a small opening that
      can be closed off air-tight
      hot plate
      water
      oven mitt

<u>Procedure</u>:

Put enough water in the metal can to cover the bottom. Place the can on the hot plate until the water has boiled (approximately two minutes). Do not put the cap on the can. Using the oven mitt, take the can off the hot plate and put on the cap. Let the can cool off. Observe what happens.

<u>Questions</u>:

1. Besides water, what was in the can? _____

WEATHER

2. What did you see coming out of the can when it was on the hot plate? _____

3. What happened to the can as it cooled? _____

4. What caused this? _____

5. What does the activity prove? _____

_____

metal can

water

hot plate

oven mitt

can after cooling

WEATHER

<u>Activity 2</u> - **The Egg in the Bottle**

<u>Materials needed</u>:

1   shelled hard boiled egg
1   bottle which has an opening a little smaller than
   the circumference of the egg
   paper, matches

<u>Procedure</u>:

Take the egg and place it over the mouth of the bottle to show that it will not go in. Now take the bottle, put the paper inside and light it with a match. As soon as the fire goes out, place the egg over the mouth of the bottle. Observe what happens.

<u>Questions</u>:

1. Why didn't the egg fall into the bottle before the paper was burned?

   _____

2. Why did the egg fall in after the paper was burned?

   _____

3. What pushed the egg into the bottle?

   _____

4. What does this activity prove?

   _____

 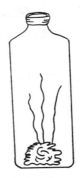 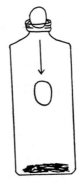

paper burning   **burnt paper**

WEATHER

Air Pressure - Activity 2
Air Force

Air pressure is the force of the atmosphere pushing on the earth. The layers of air around the earth are very heavy. The atmosphere weighs about 5.5 million billion tonnes (about 6 million billion tons). All of this air is pressing on the earth in all directions - up, down, and sideways.

Read the following information about air pressure. Write the meanings for the underlined words as they are used in the sentences.

Because of the earth's tilt the sun's rays are **absorbed** at different rates by different parts of the earth. The **tropical** zone is the source of very warm air and the **polar** regions are the source of very cold air. Large air masses move from the polar and tropical regions. The pushing and shoving of these air masses help determine our weather.

Air always moves from areas of high **pressure** to areas of low pressure. This happens because cold air which has greater **mass**, pushes with more pressure than warm air. The moving air is called wind. The greater the **difference** in pressure between two areas, the faster the wind will blow.

On weather maps, **meteorologists** use signs or codes. One kind of code they use is in the form of lines, or **isobars**, which are used to show air pressure. In all places along an isobar the **atmosphere** has the same weight. The signs used on a weather map are explained in a **key**.

There are two kinds of **barometers** - mercury barometers and aneroid barometers. Barometers rise when the pressure is High (usually giving fine weather) and fall when the pressure is Low (giving bad weather). The barometer alone does not tell the whole story but when **associated** with the **current** wind, temperature, and amount of moisture in the air, helps to **predict** tomorrow's weather.

WEATHER

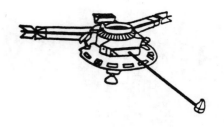

Air Pressure - Activity 3

Fronts

When the edge of a cold air mass meets the edge of a warm air mass a zone develops which is known as a front. Most of the changes in our weather take place along these fronts. There are 2 main kinds of fronts - warm fronts and cold fronts. A cold front is created when a mass of cold air moves under a mass of warm air. The cold air forces the warm air to move upward as it takes its place. These cold fronts may cause sudden changes in the weather. They usually bring heavy precipitation.

On the other hand, when a mass of warm air moves over a mass of cold air which is retreating, the warm air replaces the cold air along the surface of the ground and this creates a warm front. Warm fronts produce slower changes in the weather than cold fronts.

A Using encyclopedias and other reference materials, do some extended reading on fronts. Then compare the two by writing a paragraph about each in the space provided. Accompany your information with an illustration of each front.

Cold Fronts	Warm Fronts

Illustrate a cold front and a warm front.

 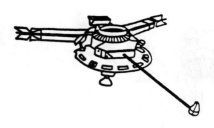

WEATHER

Air Pressure - Activity 3

Fronts

Cold Front	Warm Front

B Research the answers to the following:

1. What is an occluded front?

_____

_____

2. Name two types of occluded fronts and write a sentence or two explaining each.

_____

_____

_____

3. What is a stationary front? How does it affect the weather?

_____

_____

_____

WEATHER

Air Pressure - Activity 4

Cyclone Struck

Air is all around us. It pushes against us constantly. Fortunately, we are unable to feel this because the air inside our bodies is pushing out every bit as hard as the outside air. If this wasn't the case, we would be crushed.

The air around us is composed of small particles called molecules. When the air gets hot these molecules move about more quickly and tend to spread out. Consequently, they are unable to push down as hard. When this happens, we have what is known as a low pressure system. A low pressure area is an area in which the force of the atmosphere on the earth is relatively low. Low pressure areas usually have cloudy skies.

On the other hand, when the air gets cold, the molecules become less active and have a tendency to pack together tightly, which gives the air the power to push down very hard. When this happens we have what is known as a high pressure system. A high pressure area is an area in which the force of the atmosphere on the earth is relatively high. High pressure areas usually have clear skies.

Throughout Canada and the United States, pressure systems usually develop along the polar front. Then the cold winds and the warmer winds blow past each other, creating swirling winds known as eddies. There are two types of eddies:cyclones and anticyclones. The cyclones made by these eddies are not the same as the storms of the same name.

Cyclones form a low pressure system. Anticyclones form a high pressure system.

Using encyclopedias and other reference materials do some research on cyclones and anticyclones and write a paragraph about each.

The "pressure" is on, so be sure to do a good job!

WEATHER

Air Pressure - Activity 5

The "Value" of Pressure

What is the "Value" of pressure? To find out give each letter of the alphabet a value.

e.g. **A = 1¢ ($0.01)**   **C = 3¢ ($0.03)**
      B = 2¢ ($0.02)   **D = 4¢ ($0.04)**

Continue in this fashion until Z = 26¢ ($0.26).

The words in the clouds are all related in some way to atmospheric pressure. Write each word and give each letter its value. Then add to get a total.

e.g. **C = $0.03**
     L = 0.12
     O = 0.15
     U = 0.21
     D = 0.04
     Y = 0.25
        $0.80 or 80¢

1. **pressure**

2. **highs**

3. **lows**

4. **exerts**

5. **air**

6. **atmosphere**

7. **aneroid**

8. **barometer**

9. **systems**

10. **millibars**

What is the most expensive word in the list?_____

What is the total value of all these pressure words? _____

Now use each word in a sentence as it would relate to air pressure. Use variety in your sentences.

WEATHER

Air Pressure - Activity 6

Up, Up, and Away

Balloons are air-tight sacks. By filling them with light gases, they are able to rise. There are many different types of balloons. Children play with toy balloons. Larger balloons are used to carry passengers. <u>Weather balloons</u> measure conditions in the upper atmosphere. Approximately eight hundred observation stations around the world launch two balloons each day.

Do some research on weather balloons and answer the following questions.

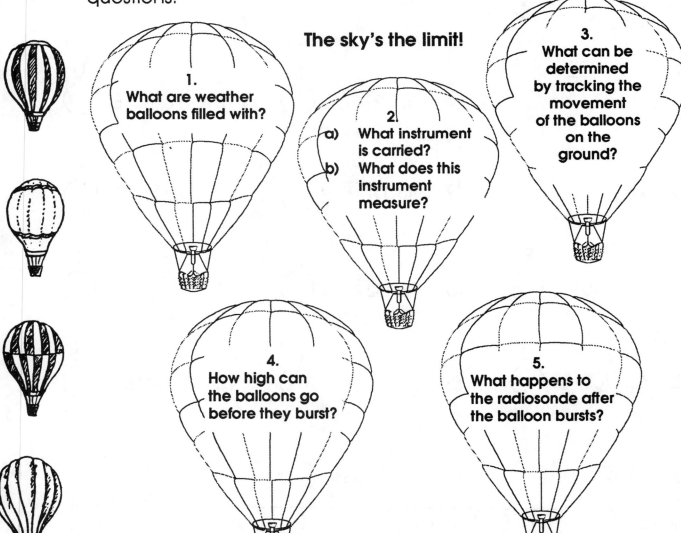

The sky's the limit!

1. What are weather balloons filled with?

2.
   a) What instrument is carried?
   b) What does this instrument measure?

3. What can be determined by tracking the movement of the balloons on the ground?

4. How high can the balloons go before they burst?

5. What happens to the radiosonde after the balloon bursts?

WEATHER

Air Pressure Activity 7

How Are You Feeling Today?

How was the air feeling when it moved from a "high" to a "low" area?

To find out the answer work out the division problems below. Write each **remainder** in the circle. Then find the remainder at the bottom of the page. Transfer the letters that appear above the remainders to the correct boxes. **The first one is done for you.**

I

1. $87\overline{)3151}$ (19)
```
      36
87)3151
   261
   541
   522
    19
```

S

2. $42\overline{)2407}$ ◯

E

3. $14\overline{)660}$ ◯

R

4. $56\overline{)2161}$ ◯

D

5. $51\overline{)3275}$ ◯

L

6. $28\overline{)1333}$ ◯

U

7. $48\overline{)3718}$ ◯

R

8. $77\overline{)3031}$ ◯

E

9. $64\overline{)2901}$ ◯

F

10. $18\overline{)529}$ ◯

S

11. $33\overline{)2537}$ ◯

G

12. $62\overline{)700}$ ◯

E

13. $26\overline{)893}$ ◯

P

14. $35\overline{)995}$ ◯

N

15. $23\overline{)256}$ ◯

E

16. $92\overline{)5366}$ ◯

The air was:

					I		
7	2	21	17	19	3	18	

15	33	09	13	29	22	28	30	11

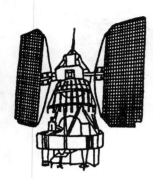

WEATHER

Air Pressure - Activity 8

Measuring the Air Pressure

The instrument used to measure air pressure is called a <u>barometer</u>.
We can make a simple barometer by using a few ordinary materials.
(Because heat is used, this activity requires adult supervision.)

Materials needed:
        1 - 500 ml (16 oz.) tin can
        1 - elastic band
        1 - large piece of balloon (to fit over can)
        2 - pieces of cardboard
            (1 piece 6.5 cm (2 1/2 in.) long by .5 cm (1/4 in.) wide)
            (1 piece 12.5 cm (5 in.) long by 2.5 cm (1 in.) wide)
    glue
    1 candle, match
    1 small bowl of ice

How to make it:

1.   Stretch the balloon across the mouth of the can. Fasten with the elastic band. It should fit tightly.

2.   Fit the larger piece of cardboard under the elastic.

3.   Fold back .5 cm (1/4 in.) at one end of the smaller piece or cardboard. Attach this to the middle of the balloon using a small amount of glue. With your pencil, draw a line on the larger piece of cardboard where the smaller piece rests.

4.   Hold the can over the candle flame. What happens to the balloon?

    _____

    Does heated air contract or expand? _____

WEATHER

Air Pressure - Activity 8

Measuring the Air Pressure

5. Now place the can in the bowl of ice. What happens to the balloon?

_____

Does the cooled air contract or expand?_____

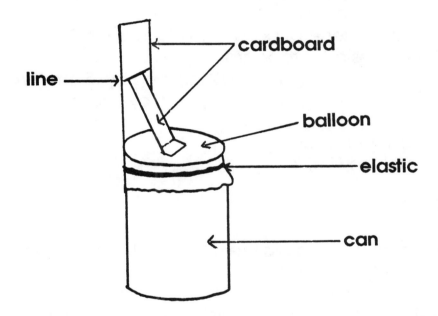

Increasing pressure is usually an indication of good weather. Falling pressure usually indicates bad weather. Watch your barometer each day. Associate the changes in the barometer reading with other weather signs such as wind direction, temperature, clouds, etc. so that you will be able to predict tomorrow's weather.

WEATHER

Moisture - Activity 1

All About Clouds

Clouds play an important part in the earth's weather. Weather changes are accompanied by constantly changing cloud formations. There are high, middle, and low clouds. Scientists have special names for clouds according to their appearance. They are:

1. **Cirrus clouds** - The prefix <u>cirro</u> - means "curl". Cirrus clouds are curly white clouds. They are high clouds and are formed entirely of ice crystals.

2. **Cumulus clouds** - The prefix <u>cumulo</u> - means "heap". Cumulus clouds are heaped-up masses of white clouds. They may float lazily across the sky or change into cumulonimbus clouds which bring thunderstorms.

3. **Stratus clouds** - The prefix <u>strato</u> - means "layer". Stratus clouds are low clouds usually seen in layers near the earth. Stratus clouds are mainly water droplets. Drizzle often falls from them.

Read more about clouds in an encyclopedia or other reference material. Then read the following sentences with information about clouds. Complete each sentence by choosing an appropriate word from the list below. The first one is done for you.

1. Clouds form from water that has ___*evaporated*___ from lakes, rivers, and oceans or moist soil and plants.

2. Condensed water vapour near the earth's surface is called
_____.

3. The process of changing water vapour into moisture by cooling is known as _____.

4. A _____ is a storm having a rotary motion and is often accompanied by a funnel-shaped cloud.

5. _____ clouds are feathery-like wispy curls of white hair.

WEATHER

6. Stratus clouds are _____ and form just above the earth.

7. The amount of water vapour in the air is called _____.

8. If a cloud forms high in the sky where it is very cold, the water vapour will change into _____.

9. _____ clouds look like a pile of cotton puffs.

10. _____ is a word that is added on to the names of clouds to show that they are rain clouds.

11. Something that helps you determine in which direction the clouds are moving is called a _____.

12. When water droplets become too big and heavy for a cloud to hold them, they fall to the ground as some form of _____, such as rain, snow, sleet, or hail.

Choose from:

cirrus, condensation,

cumulus, evaporated,

fog, humidity, ice crystals, layered,

nephoscope, nimbus, precipitation, tornado

WEATHER

Moisture - Activity 2

The Water Cycle

Our very existence is dependent on the availability of water. We drink it, cook with it, clean with it and even swim in it. We couldn't live without it! But the water we use today is basically the same water that existed billions of years ago. Imagine you may take a bath in the same water that flowed down the Amazon River!

To understand this mystery, you must realize that water flows in a continuous cycle known as the water cycle. The three most important words to remember are:

1. **evaporation** which is the changing of liquid water into a gas or vapour.

2. **condensation** which is the changing of water vapour back to a liquid form.

3. **precipitation** which is the deposition of water in any form from the air upon the surface of the earth.

In nature heat from the sun causes water to evaporate into the air from lakes, oceans, streams, the earth's soil and even puddles. The water vapour is carried up into the atmosphere by air currents. There the water vapour is cooled. The vapour hits specks of dust and condenses on them. Water drops accumulate on the dust particles and form clouds. These clouds become very heavy with water and the water will eventually fall to the earth's surface as some form of precipitation - rain, snow, sleet or hail. The water once more returns to the soil to nurture the plants and fill our streams and oceans. Soon, evaporation begins again and the cycle repeats itself over and over. Consequently, this never ending cycle keeps our water in motion through the centuries.

Activity:

Try your hand at making your own water cycle.

WEATHER

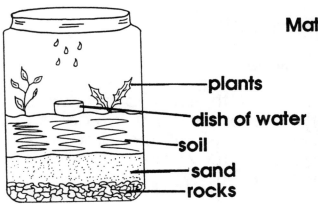

— plants

— dish of water

— soil

— sand

— rocks

Materials Needed:

1 large jar with a cover
rocks or stones
sand
soil
variety of small outdoor plants
water
a small dish

Procedure: First make a layer of small rocks in the bottom of the jar. Cover this over with a layer of sand followed by 12.5cm (5 inches) of soil. Next assemble the plants in the soil. Pack the soil firmly to be sure that the roots are well buried. Fill the small dish with water and place it inside the jar. This acts as your miniature lake. Lastly, screw the lid of the jar on tightly. Watch what happens. Allow five to seven days before writing your observations.

Observations: _____

_____

_____

_____

Creative Writing: Pretend you are a tiny drop of water. Tell your amazing story of adventure about travelling throughout the world over the past several centuries.

THE WATER CYCLE

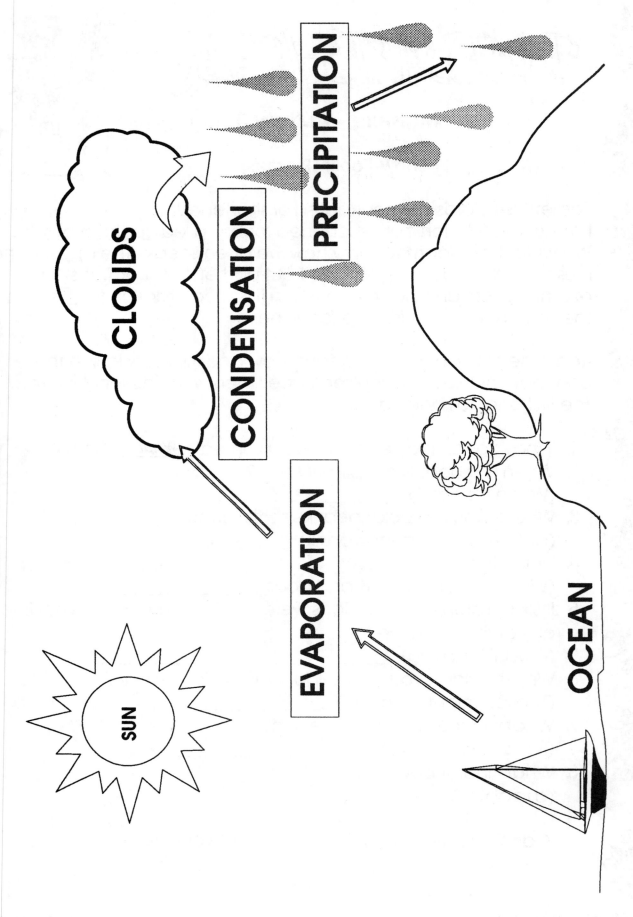

Moisture - Activity 3

Snow-Foolin' Riddles

Sometimes words are contracted or shortened. I'm, he's, you'll, don't are shortened forms called <u>contractions</u>. We write these forms to show how we often speak. The <u>apostrophe</u> is used to show that we have left out part of one word. It's, for example, uses an apostrophe when it is a contraction for <u>it is</u> as in the sentence - It's (it is) time for dinner.

Read the following riddles about snow and rain. Underline the contractions used in each sentence. Then write the longer forms. The first one has been done for you.

1. <u>What's</u> often plowed but never planted? _What is_ (snow).
2. When is a boat like a pile of snow?
   (When it's adrift) _____
3. Where would a polar bear keep its money?
   (He'd keep it in a snowbank) _____
4. When is the vet busiest?
   (When it's raining cats and dogs) _____
5. If six children and two dogs were under an umbrella, why didn't any of them get wet?
   (It wasn't raining) _____ _____
6. Why shouldn't you ever tell jokes while ice skating?
   (The ice might crack up) _____
7. What did the dirt say to the rain?
   (If this keeps up, I'll be mud) _____
8. What kind of bow can't be tied?
   (a rainbow) _____

Can you write a snow-foolin' riddle of your own?

WEATHER

Moisture - Activity 4

It's Raining Cats and Dogs

Rain, snow, hail, and sleet are different forms of precipitation. Too much precipitation may result in flooding while too little precipitation may cause a drought.

The amount of precipitation that falls on the prairies each summer is a concern to Canadians. One of Canada's major food sources is wheat. Too little or too much rain may damage the wheat crop. Listed below is the amount of rain in millimetres (mm) which fell each month in Calgary. Use this information to make a bar graph. The first month has been shaded in. Answer the questions below the graph.

Months	Precipitation
January	17 mm
February	20 mm
March	20 mm
April	31 mm
May	50 mm
June	90 mm
July	69 mm
August	57 mm
September	36 mm
October	18 mm
November	15 mm
December	15 mm

WEATHER

Calgary's Annual Rainfall

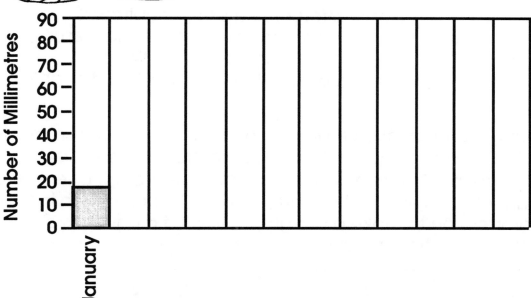

Number of Millimetres (y-axis: 0, 10, 20, 30, 40, 50, 60, 70, 80, 90)

January

Months of the Year

1. What was the <u>total</u> number of millimetres of rain which fell that year?

   _____

2. What was the <u>average</u> monthly rainfall in Calgary that year?

   _____

3. Which month had the <u>most</u> amount of precipitation?

   _____

4. Which months had the <u>least</u> amount of precipitation?

   _____ _____

WEATHER

Moisture - Activity 5

Splish Splash

Splish, splash - art in a dash! Yes, you can have a beautiful work of art by taking advantage of the pitter patter of dancing raindrops.

Using food dye or tempera paint and Q-tips dab a 21x28 cm (8 1/2" x 11") piece of paper with a variety of bold colours. Then set your paper out in the rain for several seconds. Bring it in and let it dry. On a separate piece of lined paper, write a few lines describing your rainy day masterpiece. Perhaps you could give your picture a title.

WEATHER

Moisture - Activity 6

Weird and Wacky Weather

Write an interesting paragraph about **one** of the following:

What would happen if:

1. snow was as sticky as honey
2. raindrops were as large as baseballs
3. dewdrops turned to diamonds
4. frost on your windows never melted away
5. snow was as black as tar
6. hailstones were made of marshmallows

Accompany your story with an illustration.

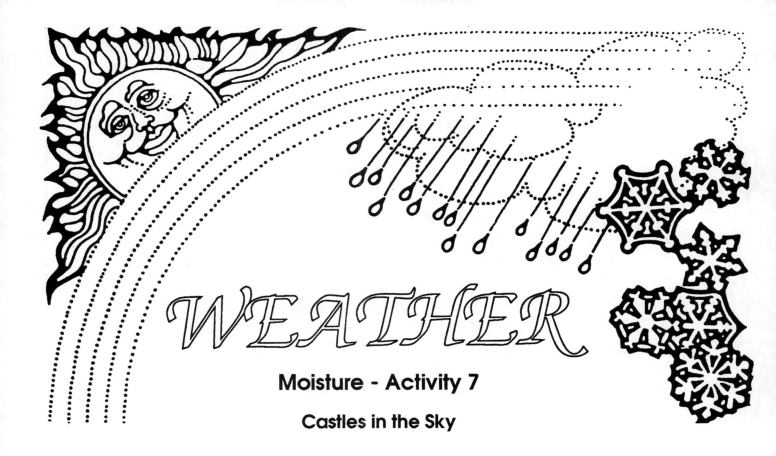

WEATHER

Moisture - Activity 7

Castles in the Sky

It's a hot, sunny summer's day. You're lying in the tall, cool grass, serene and happy as you watch the clouds lazily floating by in the blue depths of the sky above. What do you see as you study the fluffy white puffs of cotton? The faces of famous men or women, some strange animal or beast, maybe a precious little lamb or perhaps majestic castles in the sky?

Cloud watching allows the imagination to soar, the mind to wander and our creative juices to flow! The mystery of the clouds unfolds as we gaze hypnotically at their endless motions.

What shapes do you see when you go cloud watching? Take time to gaze at the clouds or recall a time when you did. Write about what you perceived to be mysteriously hidden in the skies above. What story do the clouds unfold to your imagination? This is one time when you're permitted to have "your head in the clouds!"

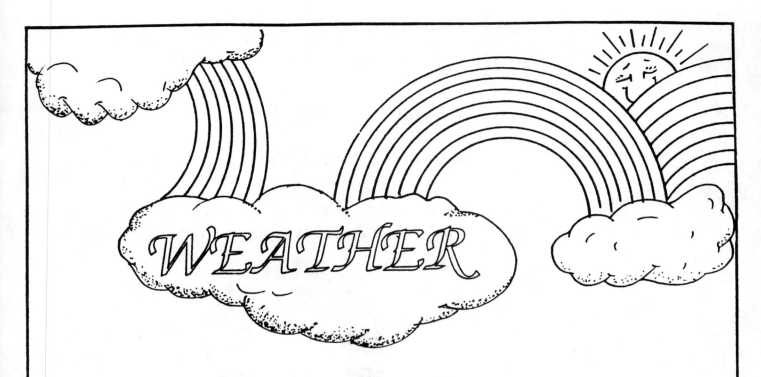

Moisture - Activity 8

Whether the Weather

Some words sound the same but have <u>different</u> spellings and <u>different</u> meanings. These words are called homonyms.

Listed below are ten sets of homonyms. Look carefully at them and use each one correctly in a sentence to show that you have an understanding of the meaning. The first word in each set must relate to weather. Use your dictionary to help you.

1. (a) rain
   (b) reign
   (c) rein

2. (a) dew
   (b) do
   (c) due

3. (a) sun
   (b) son

4. (a) hail
   (b) hale

5. (a) air
   (b) heir

6. (a) pour
   (b) pore

7. (a) weather
   (b) whether

8. (a) mist
   (b) missed

9. (a) blew
   (b) blue

10. (a) stationary (front)
    (b) stationery

WEATHER

Moisture - Activity 9

Shower Me With Words

Using this week's spelling list words, write them on the raindrops. Write a poem or story in the umbrella shape using five of your new words.

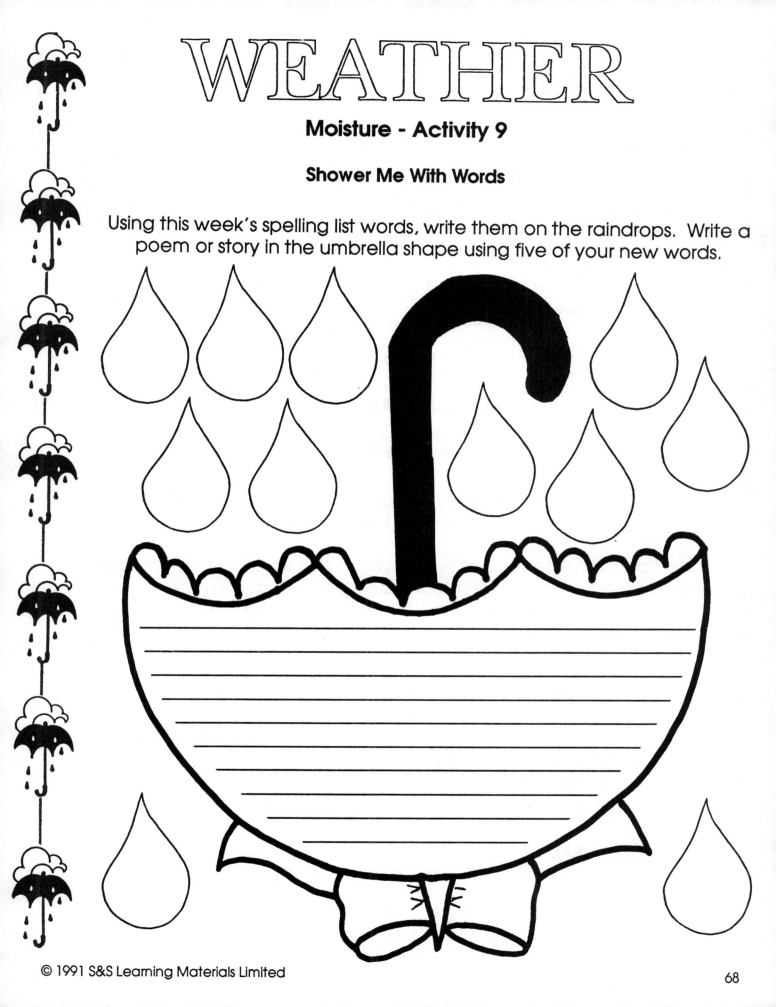

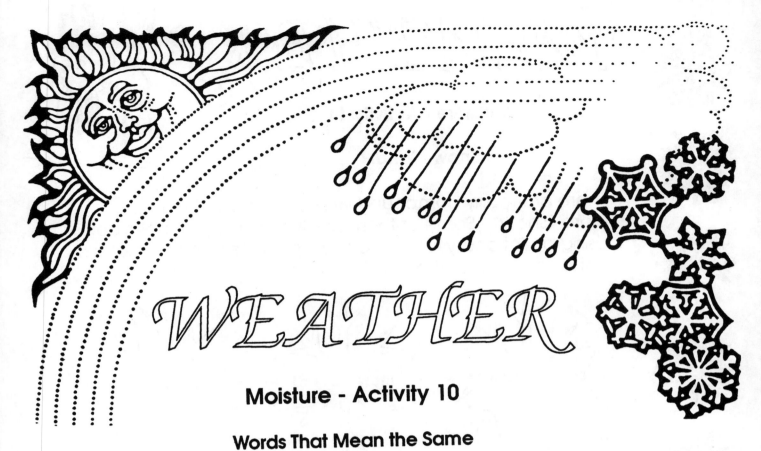

WEATHER

Moisture - Activity 10

Words That Mean the Same

Words that mean the same or almost the same are called <u>synonyms</u>.

Using a thesaurus, find and write as many synonyms as possible (at least ten) for the words below. Write the synonyms in the shapes provided. The first one has been started for you.

<u>hot</u>

<u>rain</u>

<u>cloudy</u>

<u>cold</u>

WEATHER

Moisture - Activity 11

Snow - What?

There are many compound words that contain the word "snow". Some of them are written in the shapes below. Using a dictionary, write their meaning. Tell why "snow" is a significant part of the word.

snow blindness

snow leopard

snow line

snow bunting

snowdrop

snowshoe hare

snow bound

snowy egret

snowmobile

Can you find three "snow-what" words of your own?

Moisture - Activity 12

Who is Roy G. Biv?

A <u>rainbow</u> is an arch of brilliant colours that appears in the sky when the sun shines after a shower of rain. This happens because raindrops act as tiny prisms and mirrors to break up sunlight into the colours of the <u>spectrum</u>. The colours found in the spectrum of the sun are red, orange, yellow, green, blue, indigo, and violet. The colours are always in the same order.

How are you going to remember the order?

The acronym **ROY G. BIV** is one way to remember them (<u>r</u> for red, <u>o</u> for orange, <u>y</u> for yellow, <u>g</u> for green, <u>b</u> for blue, <u>i</u> for indigo, <u>v</u> for violet).

Another way is to make up a sentence consisting of seven words
 - each one beginning with the first letter of the colours. For example:

> <u>R</u>aisins <u>o</u>n <u>y</u>ogurt <u>g</u>ive <u>b</u>ig
> <u>I</u>an <u>v</u>itamins.

Try your hand at writing a sentence of your own following this pattern.

Or perhaps you can devise another method to help you remember the colours of the spectrum.

Have a rainbow of a day!

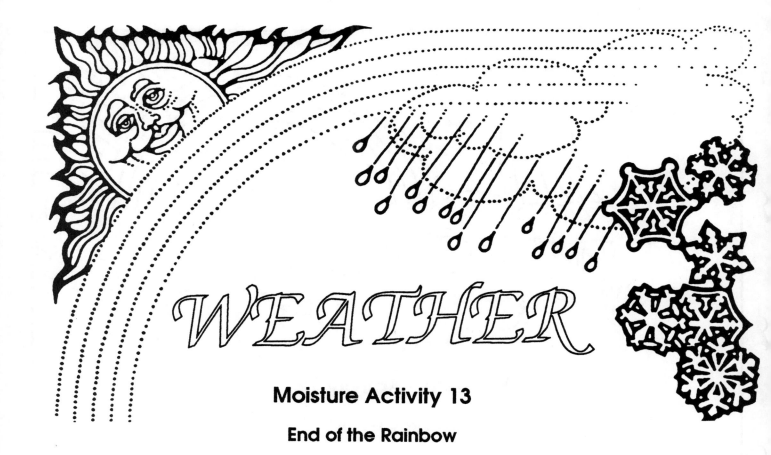

Moisture Activity 13

End of the Rainbow

<u>Somewhere Over the Rainbow</u> was a song made famous by Judy Garland. Everyone loves rainbows. Their beauty captivates the imagination of the young and the young at heart. Rainbows can be found just about everywhere we look. They adorn greeting cards, coffee mugs, wallpaper, and stickers - the list goes on! A rainbow makes me feel cheerful and happy.

A rainbow is magic and mystery folded into one. Wouldn't it be fun if we really could travel to the end of the rainbow? Would we find the famous pot of gold awaiting discovery or would we find a land where dreams come true - a Utopia where everything is beautiful and everyone is kind and loving?

What would you like to find at the end of the rainbow? I grant you magical powers to make this mysterious journey to the unknown.

Tell your story.

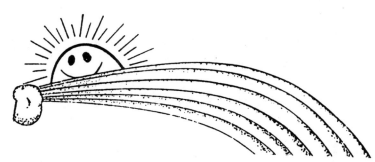

WEATHER

Moisture - Activity 14

Acid Rain

Acid rain continues to threaten our environment but we must not forget that acid snow and acid smog are just as detrimental to our health and the well being of nature in general. You may ask yourself: "How does this acidity get into the atmosphere?" Well, it starts with the emission of gases from smokestacks of fossil-fueled power plants and oil refineries as well as exhaust from automobiles. The invisible gases are mainly the oxides of sulfur and nitrogen and as they enter the air they are swept thousands of kilometers (miles) away by the winds. As time passes chemical reactions occur which convert the gases into acid-causing sulfates and nitrates. What goes up must come down so eventually the sulfuric acid and nitric acid mix with the water vapour in the clouds and return to the earth in the form of acid rain or acid snow.

In 1952 a smog covered the city of London, England for several days. During this time the death rate rose 70% and several thousand deaths were related to smog. This particular incident and others similar to it forced industries to attempt to improve the situation. What resulted was taller smokestacks to emit the gases higher into the atmosphere. Although the idea seemed logical, at the time, what actually happened was that a new problem was being created - namely - acid-rain.

Acid rain affects our lakes and streams killing off fish and other wildlife, damages our forests, our crops and our soil. It also eats away at statues, gravestones, architectural structures and automobiles. The Parliament buildings in Ottawa and the Lincoln Memorial in Washington are just two of many structures which are suffering the effects of acid rain.

On a personal basis we can all help by walking more or using a bicycle or bus service and limiting the use of the family car. On a larger scale the governments of Canada and the United States have signed an agreement to help stop this environmental problem but much more needs to be done.

WEATHER

Your assignment is to compose a letter to send to the Prime Minister of Canada (or the President of the United States) asking him to create laws that will reduce the pollution which is the cause of acid rain.

We are the people and the people must cry out for help. - Our future and the future of the entire world is at stake.

WEATHER

Moisture - Activity 15

"Fab"- ulous Weather

A fable is a narration in which animals usually speak and have other human characteristics as well. A fable ends with a moral which teaches a lesson.

Arnold Lobel wrote a fable entitled <u>The Baboon's Umbrella</u>. According to this fable a baboon was taking a walk in the jungle when he met his friend, the gibbon. The gibbon found it very unusual that the baboon would be carrying an umbrella over his head on such a bright sunny day. The baboon told the gibbon that he always takes his umbrella in case of rain but on this particular day it was stuck and he couldn't get it down. Immediately the gibbon suggested that the baboon cut holes in his umbrella to allow the sun to shine through. The baboon was very grateful for the advice and he hurried home and cut a big hole in his umbrella. The baboon was pleased that he could now enjoy the sunshine. However, soon the clouds covered the sky and rain began to fall. It came through the holes and soaked the baboon. He was most unhappy. The moral of the fable was that advice one gets from a friend is often like the weather; sometimes it's good; while sometimes it's bad!

Divide 21cm x 35cm (8 1/2" x 14") paper into 4 equal sections. Then illustrate in a sequential order four pictures that would depict what happened in "The Baboon's Umbrella".

Don't let any fair weather friends give you advice. Do a "fab"- ulous job!

WEATHER

Moisture - Activity 16

Humidity - The Hair-Raising Experience

Humidity is the amount of water vapour in the air. The greater the amount of moisture in the air, the greater the humidity. Have you ever gone for a walk on a hot, humid day? The Humidity in the air plays havoc with your hair. If you have straight hair, any attempt at curling it prior to your outing would have been done in vain. Before you know it, your hair would be as straight as a poker. On the other hand, if you have naturally curly hair or a perm your hairdo might result in frizz! Humidity can indeed be a hair-raising experience!

When the air around us cannot hold any more moisture we say that the air is saturated. The absolute humidity is the amount of water vapour in the air. Relative humidity is the amount of water vapour in the air compared to the greatest amount of water vapour it could hold at a particular temperature. Warm air can hold more moisture than cold air. Relative humidity is what concerns us the most. The higher the relative humidity, the more uncomfortable we feel. For example - If the relative humidity was 100% that would mean the air was completely saturated and is holding all the moisture it can. We begin to feel clammy because perspiration clings to us rather than evaporating into the air. The air cannot take any more moisture. The dew point is the temperature at which the air becomes saturated.

Meteorologists use an instrument called a hygrometer to help measure relative humidity. In 1783 a hygrometer was invented using human hair to predict rain. The hair would lengthen if the relative humidity was high and shorten if the relative humidity was low. So don't hesitate to make your own rain predictions. The best instrument is growing on the top of your head!

WEATHER

From the information given answer the following questions in complete sentences.

1. What is absolute humidity?

   _____

   _____

2. What is relative humidity?

   _____

   _____

3. What does it mean when we say the air is saturated?

   _____

   _____

4. If the relative humidity is high, does the air have a lot of moisture or a little moisture?

   _____

   _____

5. Why are we uncomfortable when the relative humidity is high?

   _____

   _____

6. How high can the relative humidity go? (answer in %)

   _____

7. What instrument does a meteorologist use to measure relative humidity?

   _____

8. How is our hair affected by humidity?

   _____

   _____

9. What is the dew point?

   _____

   _____

10. Which holds more moisture - warm air or cold air?

   _____

WEATHER

Moisture - Activity 17

Measuring Rainfall

The greatest rainfall amount in 24 hours in the world is 1 869.9 mm (73.62 in.) at Cilaos, La Reunion Island in the Indian Ocean, March 15, 1952. In Canada the record is held by Ucluelet, Brynnor Mines, British Columbia where on October 6, 1967, 489.2 mm (19.26 in.) of rain fell. What a splash that would make!

How can we measure rainfall? We can collect and measure rain by making an instrument called a <u>rain gauge</u>.

<u>Materials needed</u>:

1 tin can - 1.36L (48 oz.) - open at top
1 narrow straight tall glass jar (e.g. olive jar)
ruler
small measuring cup
block of wood

<u>How to make it</u>:

1. Pour 25mm (1 inch) of water into the tin can. Then pour it into the tall glass jar. The water will come much higher up the sides of this jar, and the depth can more easily be measured. Mark the water level. This will be the mark for 25 mm (1 in.) of rain. From this mark you can now measure and mark mm (tenths of inches) up to the top of the jar.

2. With the block of wood make a little platform to hold the tin can. The open top should be about 30cm (1 foot) above the ground. Put the can away from trees, buildings, etc.

3. After it rains, pour the rainwater into the tall glass jar and you can see how much has fallen

WEATHER

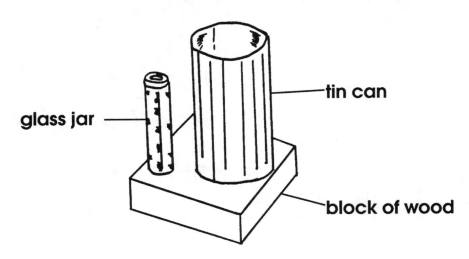

glass jar — tin can

block of wood

<u>Snowfall</u> is another common form of precipitation requiring measurement and recording. Snowfall is measured in centimetres (inches). Three centimetres would be a light snowfall. Thirty centimetres means shovelling the driveway will be a must!

Snowfall is usually measured with a ruler. Take several measurements, then find the average in order to overcome the problem of drifts.

Ten centimetres of freshly fallen snow is considered to be the equivalent of 10mm (1cm) of rain. Try melting some snow and see how accurate this is.

If snow flakes fell in different flavours which one would you choose?

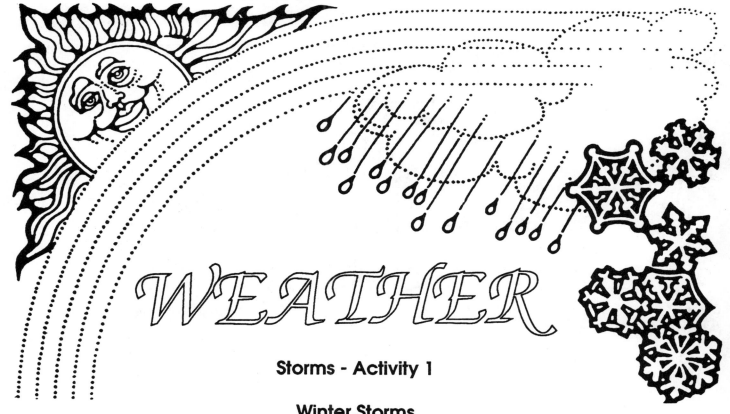

WEATHER

Storms - Activity 1

Winter Storms

Have you ever awoken on a cold winter's morning to find a menacing blizzard howling outside your bedroom window or have you ever wished you had cleats in your boots as you've gone slip, sliding away down an icy sidewalk? Ice storms and blizzards are known as winter storms.

The aftermath of a blizzard can mean fun and frolic for children playing in snowdrifts and building forts and snow sculptures. The day after an ice storm we've all admired nature's artistic touch as the ice on the heavily coated trees glistens and sparkles in the noon day sun.

However, winter storms can also be dangerous and sometimes life threatening. They can cause automobile accidents, interrupt regular transportation causing delays and cancellations. They can cause telephone wires to snap and branches of trees to fall, endangering passers-by.

Do some research on <u>ice storms</u> and <u>blizzards</u> and write five interesting facts about each.

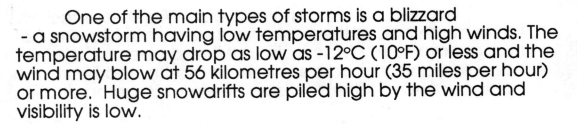

WEATHER

Storms - Activity 2

It's a Blizzard Out There!

One of the main types of storms is a blizzard - a snowstorm having low temperatures and high winds. The temperature may drop as low as -12°C (10°F) or less and the wind may blow at 56 kilometres per hour (35 miles per hour) or more. Huge snowdrifts are piled high by the wind and visibility is low.

In Canada the heaviest snowfall recorded in one day was 118.1cm (47 inches) at Lakelse Lake, British Columbia, on January 17, 1974. Imagine the snowmen and snow forts that could be made!

A Pretend **you** were there. Write a story about your adventures on that day in 1974. Was school cancelled? If so, what did you do? Were there any dangers involved or was it all fun? Use your imagination and whip up a storm! Let your ideas snowball! Remember it was a blizzard out there!

B Not so Nice Ice

If you are a hockey player or a figure skater, ice is nice. However, ice storms are not so nice. These winter storms happen when the temperature is just below freezing (0°C or 32°F). Streets and sidewalks become slippery and often cause traffic accidents. The ice can become so heavy that it can cause power lines, telephone wires, and branches of trees to break.

Pretend **you** are one of the following people and write a chilling story about what happened to you during one of the worst ice storms on record. Give lots of details about the time, the date, what you were doing, why you were out in the storm, how you dealt with it, the end result, and so on.

1. a pilot
2. an ambulance driver
3. a telephone repairman
4. a doctor
5. a policeman
6. a truck driver

WEATHER

Storms - Activity 3

Snowed Under

It was 1929. I was ten years old. Winter seemed to be much colder then and the harsh winds blowing from the harbour made my face pain as if it had been jabbed with tiny needles. January had been a hard month and February showed no signs of relief. The cold spell seemed to go on endlessly.

On February 14th, Valentine's Day, I awoke early, the whistling sound of the bitter winds filling every crack in the old wooden shingles that covered my humble home. As I peeked out through the tiny patch of window pane that Jack Frost had left unpainted, I could see the snow raging in giant swirls I jumped from my cosy bed and eagerly scraped away the frost to see what mother nature had bestowed upon us. My bedroom was on the second storey at the back of the house and to my astonishment the snow had drifted to within an arm's reach from my bedroom window. I dashed to the front windows and although the drifts were not so severe, it was quite obvious that we were indeed snowed under.

The family gradually gathered around, as each in his own turn, was awoken by the violent winds.

There was no electricity, so my father lit a fire in the fireplace and as we gathered on the old, braided rug in front of the hearth to keep warm, I couldn't help but feel a sense of peace, a cosiness that comes with being forced to return to the simple needs of life. We had a tremendous family experience. We laughed, told stories, drank hot chocolate that my Mom made by boiling water over the open fire. There was a closeness, a sense of belonging where family love radiated - something special that can better be felt rather than explained.

As evening approached, people began to dig themselves out from under and by morning life was back to normal again but the memories of being "snowed under" will always be etched in my mind and my heart.

Now write a story about a time when you and your family were "snowed under". Your story can be fact and/or fiction.

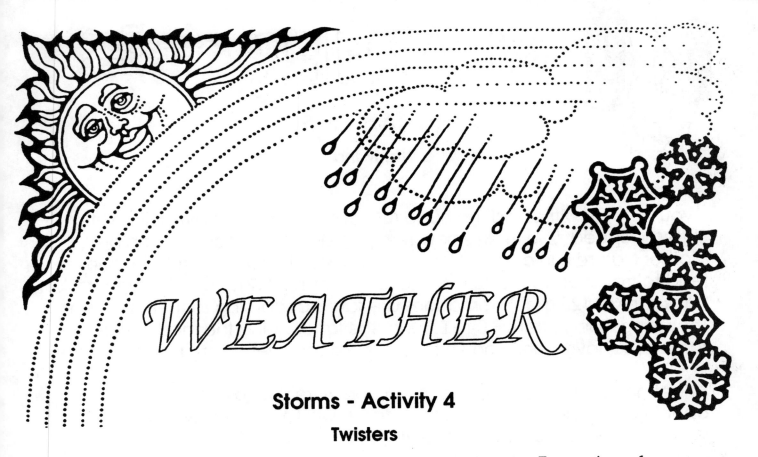

Storms - Activity 4

Twisters

Tornadoes are probably the most violent of all storms. Tornadoes form during thunderstorms and are more common in the United States than any other country, averaging about 700 a year. In Canada they are most common in Ontario and Manitoba. Canada has about 50 tornadoes a year. Tornadoes are huge wind funnels, wide at the top and narrow at the bottom. They destroy almost everything in their path - houses, cars, and dogs. Do you recall Toto and Dorothy in the movie <u>The Wizard of Oz</u> being sucked up by a tornado?

You won't get swirled away to the land of Oz, but instead you can get carried away in your library by reading information on tornadoes in reference books. Read what you can and then write <u>five interesting facts</u> about these storms.

1. _____

2. _____

3. _____

4. _____

5. _____

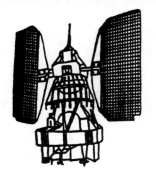

WEATHER

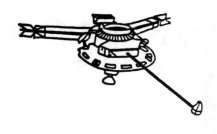

Storms - Activity 5

In a Whirlwind

If you've ever witnessed the huge funnel of a tornado advancing with extreme speed, you realize how terrifying an experience this can be! Mother Nature is in complete control and you know it. Most tornadoes tend to travel about 50-70 km/h (or 30-45 mph). Winds can be higher than 200 km/h (or 125 mph) Tornadoes are rated according to their strength. The ratings range from F 0 to F 5 with the latter being the most severe. Tornadoes have been known to lift houses completely off the ground.

Select one of the story starters given and write your own whirlwind tale about your experience with one of these whirling dervishes. Hold onto your hat - it could be swept away!

1. **We were all enjoying a fun-filled day at the beach when suddenly the sky darkened and over the horizon we could see the twister fast approaching...**

2. **We were on the airplane and off on our first family vacation to Florida. About 20 minutes before landing, the pilot announced that a tornado was sweeping the Florida coastline ...**

3. **I was walking home from the mall all by myself. Suddenly the wind was gusting, the sky grew dark and a twister came whirling across the sky. Before I knew it I was swept up in the air..**

WEATHER

Storms - Activity 6

Flash + Crash = Thunderstorm

Thunderstorms are the most common types of storms. Many many years ago people believed that thunder was the sound of the gods roaring in anger when they were displeased with the people on earth. Today we know that this is not so.

Thunder is the sound which is caused by lightning. Lightning hits the nearby air, causing it to expand. This expanding hot air has a collision with cool air. This creates sound waves that we hear as thunder. Lightning is the spark that results from the rapid movement of electrically charged particles within a cumulonimbus, or thunder, cloud. Lightning may also flash from one cloud to another, or from a cloud to a building or tree on the ground.

In Canada, the record for the highest average number of thunderstorm days each year is held by London, Ontario with 34 days. The world record is 322 days in Bogor, Indonesia.

Most people (and animals) do not like the noise thunder makes but thunder does not hurt anyone. Lightning is different. It may cause forest fires to start. It may knock over trees and telephone poles. It may kill horses and cows in fields. People may also die if they do not know how to protect themselves.

A Do some reading about lightning and/or thunderstorms. Look at the situations listed below and decide what you would do as a means of protecting yourself from lightning.

<u>**Situations**</u>   <u>**Protection**</u>

1. If you are in swimming - _____

2. If you are outside - _____

3. If you are in a car - _____

4. If you are stranded in a forest - _____

5. If you are caught in an open area - _____

WEATHER

B Decide whether the following statements are **true** or **false**. If they are false, write the sentence correctly.

1. Lightning usually strikes the highest thing around. _____

2. Buildings are protected from lightning by means of metal poles called lightning rods. _____

3. Lightning will never strike twice in the same place. _____

4. It's dangerous to leave windows and doors open during a lightning storm. _____

5. You're safer in the city than in the country during a lightning storm. _____

6. Lightning is more dangerous than thunder. _____

7. Toronto has more thunderstorms each year than Vancouver has. _____

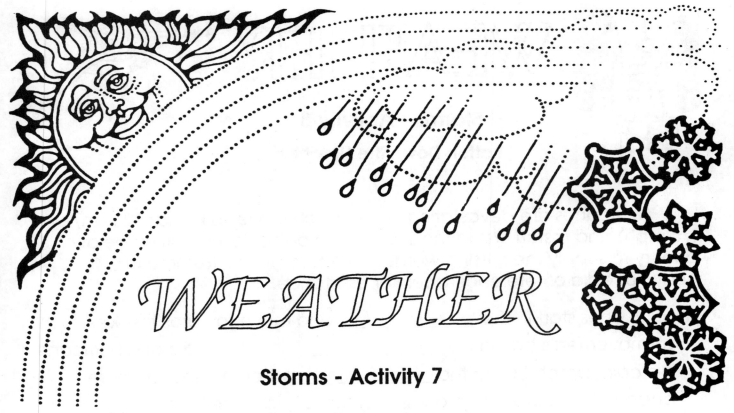

WEATHER

Storms - Activity 7

The Thunderbolt Inn

The night was dark, the wind howled and an eeriness prevailed as you wearily walked along the old, cobbled street desperately seeking a place to sleep. The hotels and motels were booked solid and you chastised yourself for not having made accommodation reservations in advance. The Thunderbolt Inn, if you could ever find it, had the only vacancy left in town.

You were getting cold now, as the sky broke and torrents of rain pounded down, chilling you to the bone. Finally you spotted the lodge and were appalled at the sight of the dilapidated old castle-like residence with crooked shutters and vines winding creepily all over the walls and windows. You shuddered with fear but as you started to walk away, you heard the roll and cracking of thunder and then lightning forked down upon the earth seeking its unsuspecting victims. You had no choice so you turned back and hastily climbed the rickety stairs and rang the doorbell. You waited for what seemed to be an eternity. Then suddenly the door jolted open and what did you see but.............

Finish this story

WEATHER

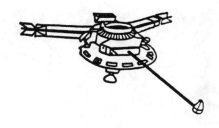

Storms - Activity 8

Batten Down the Hatches

Hurricanes are devastating winds which move as fast as 120 km/h (75 mph) and faster! Read the information on hurricanes given below and try to supply the missing words from those given. Refer to an encyclopedia or reference book for assistance.

A Hurricanes start in the _____ and move towards the west with air movements called the _____. In the middle of a hurricane is a calm patch called the _____ where things are more peaceful. Hurricanes do a vast amount of damage. They _____ homes, destroy crops and cause floods. In eastern Asia they are known as _____, while in Queensland, Australia they are called _____. In Bangladesh, hurricanes are better known as _____.

Words to choose from: tropics, willy willies, trade winds, eye, demolish, tropical cyclones, typhoons

B There's a weather poem about hurricanes that goes like this:

> **June - too soon**
> **July - stand by**
> **August - Look out**
> **September - you remember**
> **October - it's all over!**

How valid is the information in this little poem? When do most hurricanes occur? Do some research and write a paragraph reporting your findings.

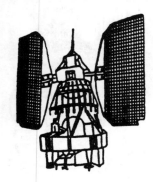

WEATHER

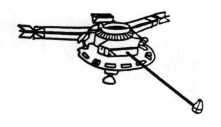

Storms - Activity 9

Name That Hurricane

Do you know a famous Diane (other than Lady Di), or a famous Donna (not Ma-donna)? What about a Betsy (besides Betsy Ross) or a famous David (not King David)?

What do Diane, Donna, Betsy, and David have in common? They are all names of hurricanes. Once a name has been used, meteorologists will not use it again, to avoid any confusion.

Hurricanes at one time were all named after girls. That changed in 1979 when boys names were used. The names alternate - girl, boy, girl, boy, etc. - and follow the letters of the alphabet in ABC order omitting the Q,U,X,Y, and Z because there are not a lot of names beginning with those letters.

A Refer to an encyclopedia, or other reference book, and write the names of **<u>five</u>** hurricanes of the 1900's. Write the year also.

1. Hurricane Flora - 1963   4. _____

2. _____   5. _____

3. _____   6. _____

B If <u>you</u> were a meteorologist and there were 7 hurricanes in 1990, what would you name them? Be creative. Don't "hurri". Maybe you know someone who is always kicking up a storm"!

A (boy)   _____

B (girl)   _____

C   _____

D   _____

E   _____

F   _____

G   _____

WEATHER

Weather Lore - Activity 1

The Groundhog

Some of what we know about the weather is scientific such as satellite photographs, radar reports, weather charts, etc. Some of it on the other hand is magical and superstitious - bones that ache before a storm, the behaviour of birds, fish, reptiles, insects and animals.

Every year on February 2, a great deal of publicity is given to the alleged foreknowledge of the groundhog. Look up the legend of the groundhog in an encyclopedia or other reference book.

A Read the information below and fill in the blanks with appropriate words found after the paragraph.

Some people believe that the groundhog or woodchuck can
_____ the weather. Groundhog Day resulted from a _____
that was brought to North America by people from Germany and
Great Britain. They believed it was a time for _____ the weather
for the next six _____. The story goes that the ground hog, or
_____ wakes up from his long winter sleep on February 2 and
sticks his head out of his home in the _____. If the sun is
_____ and the groundhog can see its _____, there will be
six more weeks of _____ weather. However, if it is a _____
day and the groundhog can not see his shadow, he apparently stays
out of his hole which indicates that _____ weather will soon come
Science has not confirmed this old story.

Words to choose from:

cloudy	custom	ground	forecasting
predict	shadow	shining	woodchuck
weeks	winter	spring	

B Write a story about Groundhog Day. Pretend you are Chuck, the groundhog, and tell how you feel about all the publicity you receive and what people expect of you. Do you like your role or do you think some other animal would be a more reliable weather forecaster? Be creative.

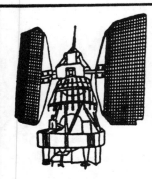

WEATHER

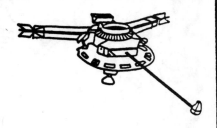

Weather Lore - Activity 2

Whether to Believe It or Not!

From the earliest times of recorded history there has been speculation about the reaction of wildlife through instinct or specialized organs to approaching weather conditions.

The cricket and the ant can both be used as natural thermometers. The frequency of the cricket's chirp depends on the air temperature - the warmer it is, the shorter is the interval between chirps. The number of chirps in eight seconds plus four will be very close to the Celsius temperature. Ants run faster as the air grows warmer and slower as the air grows colder.

Several other characteristics of animals appear to bear a relationship to future weather.

Listed in **Column A** below are some animals. In **Column B** are certain characteristics of those animals. See "whether" or not you can match them correctly.

Column A	Column B
1. farmyard hens	- become restless and edgy before a rainstorm
2. hornets and wasps	- display unruly behaviour
3. frogs and toads	- take shelter just before it rains and come out just before it stops
4. fish	- come out of their hiding places just before a rain
5. cows and horses	- repair and strengthen their webs before bad weather
6. dogs	- build their nests high before a severe winter
7. spiders	- bite better just before a storm

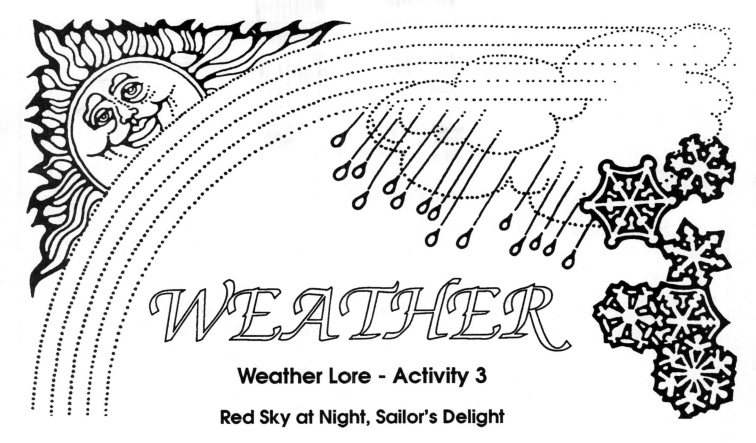

WEATHER

Weather Lore - Activity 3

Red Sky at Night, Sailor's Delight

Since the earliest days of civilization, people have tried to forecast the weather. Because technology, did not, at the time, provide sophisticated scientific instruments, farmers, fishermen and sailors would study the sky - carefully watching cloud formations and learning very quickly which winds blew cold and which ones blew warm. As a result, over the years, many sayings were developed and passed on by word of mouth. Some of the most common are listed below. Read each carefully. Then write a sentence or 2 telling whether you feel they are true or whether they are not completely reliable. Give a reason for each answer.

<u>**Weather Lore Sayings**</u>:

1. Red sky at night, sailor's delight,
   Red sky in the morning, sailors take warning.
2. When dew is on the grass, rain will never come to pass.
3. Flies will swarm before a storm.
4. Wind in the west suits everyone best.
5. A growing halo around the moon, tells of the rain that's coming soon.
6. Rain before seven, clear for eleven.

Can you think of one more weather lore saying or jingle? If so, record it below.

WEATHER

Weather Lore - Activity 4

In Like a Lion, Out Like a Lamb

I'm sure you've heard the saying about the month of March. It goes like this: if it comes in like a lion, it'll go out like a lamb. "Whether" this proverbial saying is true or not, it is still passed on as a weather lore saying and probably will be for generations to come. Why would the weather be compared to animals? Do some research on the lion and the lamb. Then write 5 characteristics of each animal.

How do you think this saying ever got started?

WEATHER

Answer Key

Temperature - Activity 1:

Part A - Answers will vary.

Part B -1. rotates, twenty-four hours;
2. orbit, year, seasons;
3. Northern, winter;
4. equator;
5. 150 000 000

Temperature - Activity 2:

1. Water freezes and turns to ice i the winter.
2. Alcohol would be used because mercury freezes at very cold temperatures.

Temperature - Activity 5:

6, 8, 4, 10, 1, 2, 5, 7, 3, 9

Temperature - Activity 6:

Part A - sunbeam, sunbonnet, sunburn, Sunburn, Sunday, sunflower, sunny, sunset, sunrise, sunshine

Part B - Answers will vary.

Temperature - Activity 10:

Part A

steady, heavy rain	light snow shower	lightning	mist
fog	intermittent moderate snow	intermittent light drizzle	steady light drizzle
heavy thunder storm	steady light snow	intermittent light rain	light rain shower
light thunderstorm with rain	H centre of high pressure	L centre of low pressure	continuous precipitation
warm front	cold front	quasi-stationary front	occlusion

Part B

1. Newfoundland
2. Quebec
3. light thunderstorm with rain
4. Manitoba, Saskatchewan, Alberta
5. Ontario
6. mist
7. New Brunswick, Prince Edward Island

Temperature - Activity 11:

1. Winnipeg
2. St. John's
3. a) 165 b) 180 c) 220 d) 245 e) 235

Wind - Activity 1:

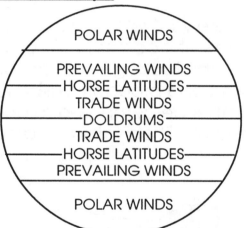

1. Prevailing Winds
2. Trade winds
3. doldrums
4. areas of light winds where many sailing ships became stalled.
5. Answers may vary.

Wind - Activity 2:

doldrums - calm area; very little wind; near the equator

monsoons - local winds that heat the land during the summer and cool the land during the winter; blow from the ocean

during the summer and toward the ocean during the winter

sirocco - a very hot, dry and dust-laden wind blowing from the northern coast of Africa across the Mediterranean and parts of Southern Europe

foehn - a warm, dry, local wind that blows down a mountainside in Europe

harmattan - a dry, dust-laden wind over the Sahara Desert that blows west or southwest to the African coast

squall - a sudden, violent gust of wind, often with rain, snow or hail

whirlwind - a current of air whirling violently round and round

wind chill - the combined cooling effect on the human body of air temperature and wind speed

gale - a very strong wind

eddies - small whirlpools or whirlwinds of water, air or smoke moving against the main current

Wind - Activity 3:
1. -24°C
2. (b)
3. -20°C; 40 kph
4. (a) -25°C; 50 kph (b) -2°C; 10 kph
5. -24°C; -37°C; -17°C; -15°C; -41°C

Chart:
1. -33°F
2. (b)
3. -5°C; 20 mph
4. (a) -5°F; 10 mph (b) 15°F; 40 mph
5. -31°F; -27°F; -33°F; -29°F; -49°F

Wind - Activity 5:
1. True
2. True
3. False (They blow from east to west.)
4. True
5. False (Wind direction is measured by a wind vane.)

6. True
7. True
8. True
9. False (Helium-filled balloons help to measure winds high above the earth's surface.)

Air Pressure - Activity 2:
absorbed - taken in

tropical - a warm area or zone

polar - a cold area or region

pressure - wind pushing against wind

mass - size

differences - a way in which the pressure is different

meteorologist - a person who reads weather maps

isobars - lines on a weather map

atmosphere - air found around the earth

key - a device used to explain signs on a weather map

barometers - instruments used to predict the weather

associated - used with

current - present, today's

predict - forecast

Air Pressure - Activity 3:
Part B
1. An occluded front is when a cold front catches up to a warm front.
2. There are two types of occluded fronts and they are cold-front occlusions and warm-front occlusions. In a cold-front occlusion, the air behind the cold front is colder than the air ahead of the warm front. In a warm-front occlusion, the air behind the cold front is warmer than the air ahead of the warm front.
3. A stationary front is one when a cold air mass and a warm air mass meet but

WEATHER

then move very little. The weather is moderate and may stay over an area for several days.

Air Pressure - Activity 5:
1. $1.21
2. $ .51
3. $ .69
4. $ .91
5. $ .28
6. $1.20
7. $ .66
8. $ .97
9. $ .90
10. $ .95

pressure; $7.28; Sentences will vary.

Air Pressure - Activity 6:
1. helium or hydrogen
2. radiosonde; measures the temperature, air pressure and humidity of the air at various altitudes
3. The direction and speed of the wind is determined by tracking the movements of the balloons.
4. They will burst at a height of 72 000 metres (90 000 feet).
5. A parachute attached to the radiosonde opens and carries it to the ground.

Air Pressure - Activity 7:
2. 57, R.13
3. 47, R.2
4. 38, R.33
5. 64, R.11
6. 47, R.17
7. 77, R.22
8. 39, R.28
9. 45, R.21
10. 29, R.7
11. 76, R.29
12. 11, R.18
13. 34, R.09
14. 28, R.15
15. 11, R.3
16. 48, R.30

The air was feeling pressured.

Moisture - Activity 1:
2. fog
3. condensation
4. tornado
5. cirrus
6. layered
7. humidity
8. ice crystals
9. Cumulous
10. Nimbus
11. nephoscope
12. precipitation

Moisture - Activity 3:
2. it is
3. he would
4. it is
5. did not; was not
6. should not
7. I will
8. cannot

Moisture - Activity 4:
1. 438
2. 36.4 mm
3. June
4. December, November

Moisture - Activity 11:
snow blindness - temporary or partial blindness from the reflection of sunlight off snow or ice

snow leopard - a wild cat of the mountains of central Asia

snow line - the line on the mountains above which there is always snow

snowbunting - a small, white finch with black and brownish markings that lives in cold, northern regions

snowdrop - a small European plant with drooping white flowers that bloom in the spring

WEATHER

snowshoe hare - a brownish hare of northern and mountainous areas of North America that turns white in the winter

snowbound - shut in by snow; snowed in

snow egret - a white heron or egret of temperate and tropical America with black legs and yellow feet

snowmobile - a tractor or other vehicle used in snow, some having skis or runners in front

Moisture - Activity 16

1. Absolute humidity is the amount of water vapour in the air.
2. Relative humidity is the amount of water vapour in the air compared to the greatest amount of water vapour it could hold at a particular temperature.
3. The air is saturated when it can no longer hold anymore moisture.
4. It has a lot of moisture.
5. The moisture makes us feel clammy because perspiration clings to us.
6. It can be 100 percent.
7. He uses a hygrometer.
8. Our hair will go straight as a poker or very curly.
9. The dew point is the temperature at which the air becomes saturated.
10. Warm air can hold more moisture.

Storms - Activity 6:
Part A
1. Get out quickly.
2. Take shelter in a house or building.
3. Stay inside; do not touch any metal parts.
4. Take cover beneath low shrubs or groups of trees the same size.
5. sit or crouch down.

Part B
1. True
2. True
3. False (The Empire State Building has been struck 9 times in 20 minutes.)
4. False (Closing windows and doors will keep out the rain but otherwise has practically no effect on lightning.)
5. True
6. True
7. True

Storms - Activity 8:
Part A - tropics; trade winds; eye; demolish; tropic cyclones; willy willies; typhoons.

Part B - Answers will vary.

Storms - Activity 9:
Part A
2. Hurricane Betsy, 1965
3. Hurricane Beulah, 1967
4. Hurricane Camille, 1969
5. Hurricane Agnes, 1972
6. Hurricane Fifi, 1974
7. Hurricane Alicia, 1983
8. Hurricane Diane, 1955
9. Hurricane Audrey, 1957
10. Hurricane Donna, 1960

Part B - Answers will vary.

Weather Lore - Activity 1:
Part A - predict; custom; forecasting; weeks; woodchuck; ground; shining; shadow; winter; cloudy; spring

Part B - Answers will vary.

Weather Lore - Activity 2:
6, 5, 1, 3, 7, 2, 4

WEATHER

WEATHER

 # WEATHER

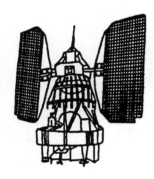 WEATHER